A DAY THAT MADE HISTORY

THE EASTER RISING

Nathaniel Harris

Dryad Press Limited   London

F

Contents

THE EVENTS

THE INVESTIGATION

Acknowledgments

The author and publishers thank the following for their kind permission to reproduce copyright illustrations: BBC Hulton Picture Library, pages 23, 39, 40, 60; George Morrison, pages 3, 4, 5, 6, 7, 11, 18, 22, 25, 26, 27, 28, 32, 33, 34, 43, 54, 58, 59, 61; courtesy of the National Library of Ireland, pages 13, 41, 42, 46, 49, 55; Photo Images Ltd, Dublin, page 62 and the front cover; Ulster Museum, page 52. The map on pages 20-21 was drawn by R.F. Brien. The pictures were researched by David Pratt.

The "Day that Made History" series was devised by Nathaniel Harris.

© Nathaniel Harris 1987. First published 1987.
Typeset by Tek-Art Ltd, Kent, and printed by R.J. Acford Ltd, Chichester, Sussex
for the publishers, Dryad Press Limited, 8 Cavendish Square, London W1M 0AJ

ISBN 0 8521 9718 7

21123896 W

TS

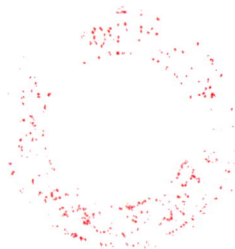

THE
EVENTS

"The GPO – Charge!"

Marching up Sackville Street

The rising began in the centre of Dublin, at a time when most of the city was on holiday. At almost exactly noon on Easter Monday – in 1916 it fell on April 24th – the First Army of the Irish Republic came marching up Sackville Street, past the shops and hotels that lined the city's main thoroughfare. Then, at a word of command, the soldiers came to a halt outside the General Post Office.

In reality, this contingent of the First Army consisted of a motley few dozen men and three or four motor vehicles including an ordinary Ford tourer. The "Army" itself was a creation of that Easter Monday, bringing together the men of two para-military organizations dedicated to the overthrow of British rule in Ireland – the nationalist Irish Volunteers and

The Irish Volunteers, a part-time nationalist army, provided most of the rebel troops who took part in the Easter Rising. The photograph, which dates from 1915, shows Volunteers drilling.

the smaller Citizen Army, which was drawn from the ranks of working-class socialists and trade unionists. Most of the "soldiers" were dressed in civilian clothes, although they had tried to make themselves look more warlike by decking themselves out with bandolier straps, riding breeches, puttees, holsters and other military-style accessories. Only a small minority wore the greyish-green uniforms and peaked caps of the Irish Volunteers, or the darker green outfits and slouch hats of the Citizen Army. The men presented a curious, even eccentric spectacle, since they were laden with a variety of weapons ancient and modern – even some pikes – and a mysterious collection of tins, ropes, hammers, picks and other pieces of equipment that seemed distinctly out of place on a "parade".

A parade is what most bystanders, including policemen and British officers, believed the marching column to be: everybody was used to the drilling and manoeuvres carried out by the republicans, who had been "playing at soldiers" so long that many people no longer took them seriously as a threat to British rule. No doubt that was why these rebels in arms were able to leave their headquarters at Liberty Hall and march into Sackville Street without causing the slightest alarm.

The leaders

At the head of the "Army" strode its three leaders, shoulder

James Connolly in about 1910. Connolly became leader of the Irish Transport and General Workers' Union in 1914. A committed socialist, he formed the small Irish Citizen Army as a defence force after the transport workers' strike of 1913-14, during which the police had behaved with great brutality. But Connolly was also passionately eager to help Ireland throw off British rule, and it was largely because of his demands for action that the rising took place when it did.

Joseph Mary Plunkett in 1914. Plunkett, though stricken with tuberculosis, planned the military strategy of the Easter Rising and took part in the assault on the GPO.

to shoulder. There can have been few rebellions such as this one, in which a trade unionist and two poets led the insurgents into action. The man in the centre, James Connolly, was in civilian life the secretary of the Irish Transport and General Workers' Union. A burly figure with a heavy moustache, he wore the uniform of the Citizen Army, of which he was the leader. Connolly had been appointed the rebels' operational commander on the basis of his service in the British army and his study of street-fighting tactics; he was to direct the republican forces during the actual hostilities.

The man on Connolly's left was an extraordinary figure, slender, sickly, bespectacled and beringed; his throat was bandaged as a result of an operation, and he was in fact dying of tuberculosis. This was Joseph Mary Plunkett, literary editor and poet. He was an amateur strategist with no military experience, but it was nevertheless he who had worked out the overall plan for the rising.

Patrick Pearse, schoolteacher and poet, had few pretensions as a commander or organizer, but he did possess the power to inspire men. His eloquent speeches had stirred up anti-British feeling, and his mystical poetry, with its praise of

5

Patrick Pearse in 1915, recruiting for the Irish Volunteers at Dolphin's Barn, Dublin.

blood-sacrifice, had caught the imagination of many youthful republicans. Although only the inner ring of rebels knew of it, Pearse had been elected first president of the Irish Republic-to-be and nominal commander-in-chief of its forces. As such, he marched at the front of the column, on Connolly's right.

At some distance behind the marching column, on the pavement, came two other committed republican leaders. One was 58-year-old Tom Clarke, father-figure to the revolutionists of the new generation, who had won his authority through spending fifteen years in British prisons. The other, Sean MacDermott, was a gifted and charming young organizer and political "fixer" who might in other circumstances have become a successful parliamentary careerist. The two men travelled slowly, for MacDermott was a victim of polio and could only limp along with the help of a stick.

Into action

The General Post Office in Sackville Street was a massive

structure in the classical style, entered through an imposing six-columned portico that thrust out across the entire width of the pavement in front of the building. The rebels had decided to make it their headquarters because it was big enough to hold large numbers of men and quantities of equipment, and strong and compact enough to withstand an enemy assault for a very long time. It also appeared to be strategically well-placed in the heart of the city, from which Connolly could maintain communications with the other strongpoints that the rebels were planning to seize at almost the same moment.

When his tiny army had come to a halt outside the Post Office, Connolly, in a voice thick with emotion, gave the order: "Left turn! GPO – Charge!"

Although it was a bank holiday, the Post Office was open and doing a fair amount of business. But after an initial moment of shock at being ordered out of the building by armed men, the queues melted away. Clerks jumped over the counters, and staff and customers made a rush for the doors,

Sackville Street in 1914. This photograph of Dublin's main thoroughfare shows two of its best-known landmarks: the six-columned entrance to the General Post Office, which became the rebel head-quarters, and the Nelson Pillar, a 40-metre-high column surmounted by a statue of the famous admiral. The Pillar, like the GPO, survived the Easter Rising and the "troubles" of subsequent years, only to be blown up in 1966.

encouraged by a couple of shots from guns fired accidentally by nervous or inexpert rebels. Their inexperience was responsible for several minor accidents in the course of the day, with weapons and also with the tin cans they had brought; these were in fact home-made bombs, which often proved to be more dangerous to their makers than they were to the British army.

Only two of the crowd in the Post Office were detained and made prisoners, a British lieutenant and a Dublin policeman. When the ground floor had been cleared, the rebels stacked most of their weapons and equipment in the middle of the room. Then they set about preparing their defences. They smashed all the windows and loopholed them – that is, piled up furniture, books and anything else they could lay hands on, so that only a narrow slit remained through which the defenders could fire without exposing themselves. In time they also barricaded the entrance, using "sandbags" packed with coal dust from the basement fuel store.

Meanwhile another of the republican leaders had reached the Post Office. This was Michael O'Rahilly, better known as The O'Rahilly, the courtesy title given to a clan chief. The O'Rahilly was a large, expansive character, but on this occasion his relations with Pearse and the rest were strained. Like many of the Volunteers' leaders, he had opposed the rising, on the grounds that it was hopelessly ill-timed, and only a day or so earlier he had done everything he could to stop it. Yet when he realized that some men were certain to come out on the Easter Monday, he had surprised everybody by deciding to join them. Having spent years working to challenge British rule, he felt that he could not stand aside now. Or, as he himself put it earlier in the morning, on arriving at Liberty Hall, "I helped to wind this clock: I might as well hear it strike."

On his arrival at the GPO, The O'Rahilly pointed out to Pearse that, carried away by their zeal for constructing defence-works, the rebels had not yet occupied and searched the upper storeys. This was a serious omission, since the telegraph office was situated on the first floor, and might at that very moment be transmitting news of the rising to the British authorities elsewhere. Pearse hastily ordered a Volunteer named Staines to clear the rest of the building, and he went upstairs accompanied by half-a-dozen men armed with revolvers and automatics. On the way they met a group of girls from the telegraph office coming down. Like most Dubliners on that day, the girls had little sympathy with the rebels and were not afraid of showing it; only one, who knew Staines, called out encouragingly "Hello, Micheál! That's the stuff to give them!"

But neither she nor the other girls warned Staines of what lay ahead on the landing outside the telegraph office. When they got there, the rebel party heard a sound behind them and turned quickly. They found themselves face to face with seven British soldiers who carried rifles. One or more of the rebels opened fire, a soldier fell, and – to the amazement of the rebels – his comrades all raised their hands and surrendered. Their behaviour became easier to understand when Staines discovered that their weapons were not loaded and they had not been issued with ammunition; they had been assigned to guard the GPO, but their superiors evidently considered that their presence alone would be enough to prevent trouble. Fortunately the man who had been hit – a Scottish sergeant – proved to have sustained no more than a bullet-graze on his forehead. He was carried off to the hospital two blocks away in Jervis Street, while his men were taken to join the other prisoners.

The rest of the building was occupied without incident, although the woman in charge of the telegraph office (as it happened, she was another Scot) lingered for some time before she was persuaded to leave her post; she probably did so only when she realized there was no chance of tapping out an alert to the British forces. After her departure, the only woman in the GPO was Winifred Carney, Connolly's devoted secretary, who had set up her typewriter on the main counter, ready to copy documents and instructions as required. At this stage, Connolly was in touch with a number of the rebel positions elsewhere in Dublin, receiving reports brought by despatch riders on motor cycles. Later, when this became too dangerous, messages were carried to and fro on bicycles by non-combatants, mostly Fianna Boys belonging to the Fianna na h'Eireann, a nationalist boy scouts organization, and young members of the Cumann na mBan (League of Women).

Birth of a republic

A few minutes after the attack on the Post Office, Connolly sent a useful officer named Sean T. O'Kelly to fetch a brown paper parcel from Liberty Hall. It contained two flags, one of them all green, with a gold harp and the words "Irish

Republic" in gold and white lettering, the other a tricolour with green, white and orange stripes. The British flags flying from the roof of the GPO were hauled down, and the new symbols of independent Irish nationhood were run up on the flagpoles above the corners of the building; between them, however, lay a less easily removed reminder of British authority, the royal arms carved inside the large triangular pediment above the portico.

The raising of the Irish flags was followed by a symbolic event of even greater significance. Accompanied by an armed escort, Pearse and Connolly emerged from the GPO and stood on the steps to address the crowd that had gathered in front of the building. Pearse was pale and nervous, perhaps because he was aware that his audience was not in a sympathetic frame of mind. Dubliners were famous for their irreverent, derisive wit, and there was a real danger that one or two cruelly clever hecklers would use their talents to mar the occasion. Pearse read out a few words of Gaelic, the ancient Irish language that nationalists hoped to revive, and then reverted to English, the only language spoken and understood by most Irishmen. Slowly he declaimed the entire text of a document in which the "Provisional Government of the Irish Republic" addressed the citizens whose allegiance it demanded.

This stirring proclamation was mainly the work of Pearse himself, with some help from his colleagues. It began:

> "Irishmen and Irishwomen: In the name of God and of the dead generations from which she receives her old tradition of nationhood, Ireland, through us, summons her children to her flag and strikes for her freedom."

Responsibility for the rising was proudly claimed by the "secret revolutionary organization, the Irish Republican Brotherhood", and the "open military organizations, the Irish Volunteers and the Irish Citizen Army". The proclamation asserted that the rebels would be supported by Ireland's "exiled children in America" (the large Irish-American population in the United States) and by "gallant allies in Europe" (the Germans, currently in the middle of a World War against the British). After rehearsing the long history of Irish revolts against British domination, Pearse announced the formation of the Provisional Government and declared that:

The proclamation of an Irish Republic was read out to Dubliners by Patrick Pearse on Easter Monday, 1916; copies were pasted up all over the city.

POBLACHT NA H EIREANN.

THE PROVISIONAL GOVERNMENT
OF THE
IRISH REPUBLIC
TO THE PEOPLE OF IRELAND.

IRISHMEN AND IRISHWOMEN: In the name of God and of the dead generations from which she receives her old tradition of nationhood, Ireland, through us, summons her children to her flag and strikes for her freedom.

Having organised and trained her manhood through her secret revolutionary organisation, the Irish Republican Brotherhood, and through her open military organisations, the Irish Volunteers and the Irish Citizen Army, having patiently perfected her discipline, having resolutely waited for the right moment to reveal itself, she now seizes that moment, and, supported by her exiled children in America and by gallant allies in Europe, but relying in the first on her own strength, she strikes in full confidence of victory.

We declare the right of the people of Ireland to the ownership of Ireland, and to the unfettered control of Irish destinies, to be sovereign and indefeasible. The long usurpation of that right by a foreign people and government has not extinguished the right, nor can it ever be extinguished except by the destruction of the Irish people. In every generation the Irish people have asserted their right to national freedom and sovereignty; six times during the past three hundred years they have asserted it in arms. Standing on that fundamental right and again asserting it in arms in the face of the world, we hereby proclaim the Irish Republic as a Sovereign Independent State, and we pledge our lives and the lives of our comrades-in-arms to the cause of its freedom, of its welfare, and of its exaltation among the nations.

The Irish Republic is entitled to, and hereby claims, the allegiance of every Irishman and Irishwoman. The Republic guarantees religious and civil liberty, equal rights and equal opportunities to all its citizens, and declares its resolve to pursue the happiness and prosperity of the whole nation and of all its parts, cherishing all the children of the nation equally, and oblivious of the differences carefully fostered by an alien government, which have divided a minority from the majority in the past.

Until our arms have brought the opportune moment for the establishment of a permanent National Government, representative of the whole people of Ireland and elected by the suffrages of all her men and women, the Provisional Government, hereby constituted, will administer the civil and military affairs of the Republic in trust for the people.

We place the cause of the Irish Republic under the protection of the Most High God, Whose blessing we invoke upon our arms, and we pray that no one who serves that cause will dishonour it by cowardice, inhumanity, or rapine. In this supreme hour the Irish nation must, by its valour and discipline and by the readiness of its children to sacrifice themselves for the common good, prove itself worthy of the august destiny to which it is called.

Signed on Behalf of the Provisional Government,

THOMAS J. CLARKE.
SEAN Mac DIARMADA,   THOMAS MacDONAGH.
P. H. PEARSE,   EAMONN CEANNT,
JAMES CONNOLLY.   JOSEPH PLUNKETT.

"In this supreme hour the Irish nation must, by its valour and discipline and by the readiness of its children to sacrifice themselves for the common good, prove itself worthy of the august destiny to which it is called."

The proclamation was signed by the seven members of the Provisional Government, five of whom were in the GPO:

Pearse, Connolly, Plunkett, Clarke, and Sean MacDermott, whose name appeared in its Gaelic form, MacDiarmada. The other signatories, Ceannt and MacDonagh, were commanding strongpoints elsewhere in Dublin.

Pearse's speech was not a success. There was no serious heckling, but neither was there any enthusiasm; the few feeble cheers that greeted the proclamation merely seemed to emphasize the indifference with which the majority received it. When it was over, Connolly and Pearse briefly shook hands. Connolly said "Thanks be to God, Pearse, we have lived to see this day"; and the two men withdrew into the Post Office. Charged with pasting up printed copies of the proclamation, Sean T. O'Kelly discovered that none of the necessary materials had been provided. He and his men had to break into several shops and take the flour, brushes and buckets needed to do the job. They made a paste in the basement of the GPO and then set to work, putting up about two hundred notices that day. In Sackville Street itself, the proclamation appeared on the portico columns of the GPO, and on the nearby walls. One copy was placed on the ground in front of Nelson's Pillar – the Dublin equivalent to Nelson's Column in Trafalgar Square – which stood in the middle of Sackville Street just a few metres from the Post Office. A number of people stopped to read the printed sheet in a perfunctory way, but most of the crowd continued to take a sporting rather than a serious political interest in events at the GPO. Their ranks thinned a little as the prospect of more broken glass or speechifying faded, although the street remained thronged. The proclamation of a republic, later to be seen as a landmark in modern Irish history, was, to those who participated in it, an occasion that seemed to have fallen rather flat.

Skirmish in Sackville Street

Hopes and fears

When the rebels had mustered at Liberty Hall on Easter Monday morning, the turnout by the largest military organization, the Irish Volunteers, had been disappointingly small. This was not really surprising, since its leaders had disagreed about the desirability of a rising over Easter, and conflicting orders had caused a good deal of confusion. Many, who might otherwise have taken part, remained uncertain what to do, or simply failed to hear the news in time; and since the insurrection took place on the holiday Monday, many potential rebels – like many British soldiers – left Dublin early that morning in order to attend the popular Fairyhouse horse races. Although new recruits did present themselves during the day as word of the rising spread, it soon became

clear that in Dublin the rebels could only hope to realize a fraction of their possible manpower. In the event, the fighting throughout the city during the great Easter Rising in Dublin was done by about 1600 men – some 1400 Irish Volunteers, 200 members of the Citizen Army and a handful of volunteers from another group, the Hibernian Rifles.

Since the people of Dublin remained passive or even hostile, the rebels' lack of manpower put severe limits on what they could hope to achieve. And of course it also meant that they were doomed to a swift defeat unless help arrived from outside. From time to time, beginning on the Monday afternoon, wild rumours of German landings, and of rebel victories in the provinces, buoyed up the hopes of the men in the GPO. But these were mostly products of wishful thinking. Pearse and the other leaders – though not the rank and file – knew that plans to obtain aid from Germany had badly miscarried. And although communications with the rest of Ireland were poor (since the rebels failed to seize the telephone exchange), all the information that did come to hand was anything but encouraging: Ireland seemed to have ignored the call to take up arms against the oppressor. The 1600 men of the republican "army" would almost certainly have to stand alone against the might of the British Empire – an empire already mobilized for war and battle-hardened in Flanders.

This prospect daunted the leaders less than might have been expected. They may have dreamed of victory – of holding out for several months until Germany won the World War and called them to an honoured place at the Peace Conference. But they realized that defeat and death were far more likely, and were prepared to sacrifice themselves in the conviction that their actions would reawaken Ireland. Pearse had an intense belief in the value of blood-sacrifice which most people would now find rather unattractive; he welcomed the coming of the World War, and roundly declared that "Bloodshed is a sanctifying thing, and the nation which regards it as the final horror has lost its manhood"; and "Life springs from death; and from the graves of patriot men and women spring living nations." The socialist Connolly was far less mystically inclined than Pearse, but he too believed that a dramatic gesture was needed to arouse the masses. When he was about to leave Liberty Hall on Easter Monday morning, he stopped to speak to his friend William O'Brian. "We're going out to be slaughtered, Bill," he remarked. "Is there no hope at all?" asked O'Brian.

"None whatsoever," replied Connolly with disconcerting cheerfulness.

Barricading and provisioning the GPO

Connolly himself can have had little time for reflection over the next few hours, as he hurried to complete the rebel defences against a British attack that might begin at any moment. On the march up Sackville Street Connolly had sent small detachments to occupy Hopkins the jeweller's and Kelly's gun store, the corner shops commanding Bachelor's Walk, Eden Quay and the O'Connell Bridge. Later in the afternoon, other small parties were sent to take over such prominent buildings as the Metropole Hotel, just across Prince's Street from the GPO, the Manfield boot factory and Eason's bookshop on the corner of Abbey Street, and, on the other side of Sackville Street, the Imperial Hotel, Marconi House and the tall Dublin Bread Company with its curious little oriental-style tower; since the Imperial had figured as a capitalist stronghold during a great strike in 1913, Connolly had the Irish socialist banner, the Starry Plough, run up on the roof of the hotel. Despite all the shortcomings of the rebels' training and organization, Irish sharpshooters on the roofs of these and other buildings were to give a good account of themselves in the days to come.

Meanwhile a barricade was constructed across the near end of Abbey Street, on the line of march from Amiens Street railway station, where British reinforcements were expected to arrive in readiness for an attack on the Post Office. Giant rolls of newsprint, pieces of furniture and other objects were piled up across the roadway and bound together with wire to make a bullet-proof barrier that would be as awkward and dangerous as possible to climb. Among the items requisitioned for this purpose were a number of brand-new bicycles from a nearby shop. These attracted the attention of the bystanders, who swarmed over the barricade and tried to disengage the bicycles from the heap. They were only persuaded to retreat when the rebels fired a volley of shots over their heads.

This incident did nothing to help the rebels' popularity. Understandably, ordinary Dubliners failed to see much difference between the way in which the republican army requisitioned goods and the kind of thieving done by common criminals. People either condemned such actions as immoral;

or they resented not being allowed to join in; or they managed to feel both emotions simultaneously. Some of the rebels also had qualms. O'Kelly, who had been ordered to commandeer as much bread and milk as he could lay hands on, felt guilty about taking shopkeepers' goods at gunpoint, and giving in return IOUs in the name of a republican government that might have ceased to exist by the following day. Nonetheless the task was accomplished, and a steady procession of vans – commandeered, like the foodstuffs they carried – was soon passing through the Prince's Street entrance to the Post Office.

Though the crowd had not yet got out of hand, its numbers were large enough to disturb law-abiding people, especially since the Dublin Metropolitan Police had evidently withdrawn from the scene. (This was only prudent: as servants of the Crown they were regarded as enemies by the rebels, and were liable to be shot if they tried to interfere.) In their place, a group of priests devised an ingenious scheme to clear Sackville Street. Correctly assuming that no Catholic Dubliner would get himself into a collision with a man of the cloth, they linked hands to form a chain across the breadth of the street, and then marched steadily along its entire length. But though everyone fell back respectfully, most people simply took evasive action, retreating into one of the side streets and then re-emerging as the line of black-robed clerics passed by them.

The Lancers

The street was cleared much more effectively when someone started shouting "The Lancers! The Lancers are coming!" At the prospect of being ridden down by horsemen, the crowd melted away, leaving an empty street in which an upturned tram marked the place where the rebels had begun to set up a new barricade. Sharpshooters on the roof of the GPO had been the first to spot a troop of these elite British cavalrymen approaching from the north, in perfect formation and as ceremonially stiff as if they were on parade. At Parnell's monument they halted briefly, then fanned out. When their commanding officer, Colonel Hammond, gave the order, the Lancers advanced to the attack with pennants flying. They must have presented a splendid sight – like the doomed Light Brigade at Balaclava. It is hard to imagine what Hammond supposed he could achieve: perhaps he believed that the rebels were no more than a group of rowdies who would run at the mere sight of proper soldiers. In reality, Hammond's decision was so foolhardy as to be potentially suicidal, since his men would have to charge down an open street, without any possibility of taking cover, while an unknown number of concealed enemies riddled them with bullets from all sides.

Before a shot was fired, an almost comic incident occurred. A party of Volunteers from the Dublin suburb of Rathfarnham turned into Sackville Street just as the cry went up that the Lancers were advancing. These men, like so many other Volunteers, had only been informed of the rising during the morning, but they had responded quickly, assembling at the Yellow House pub in Rathfarnham and then taking a tram into the centre of the city. Now, ill-armed and without the slightest experience of action, they found themselves caught in the open street while British cavalry thundered down on them. They bolted across the main road and into Prince's Street, where friendly hands pulled them through the Post Office windows, although jagged edges of the broken glass, still embedded in the frames, inflicted some unpleasant gashes in the process. The comic aspect of the scene was spoiled by the fact that two Rathfarnham men failed to get through the window in time and were badly wounded – one by his own rifle, which went off accidentally, the other by a stray bullet that was probably aimed at the British by a sniper on the other side of the road.

In the event, the Lancers themselves did not fire a shot. As they neared the Post Office, one of the rebels lost patience and disobeyed Connolly's command not to fire until the order was given. Once this had happened, the other rebels joined in, and the chance of annihilating the horsemen with a devastating volley at close quarters was lost. However, this first ragged burst of shooting brought down four Lancers and threw the rest into confusion. The British troops were already retreating when the rebels hurriedly let loose with a second, less effective, volley which only succeeded in killing two of the soldiers' horses. Of the four men who had been hit, three were already dead; the fourth, mortally wounded, was taken away soon afterwards by an ambulance. Apart from the casualties among the Rathfarnham contingent, the rebels lost only one man, a sniper who had been stationed in a building opposite the Post Office, from which the bullet that accidentally killed him must have come.

Seeing the Lancers disappearing into the distance, Connolly's men sent up a cheer: they were less conscious of

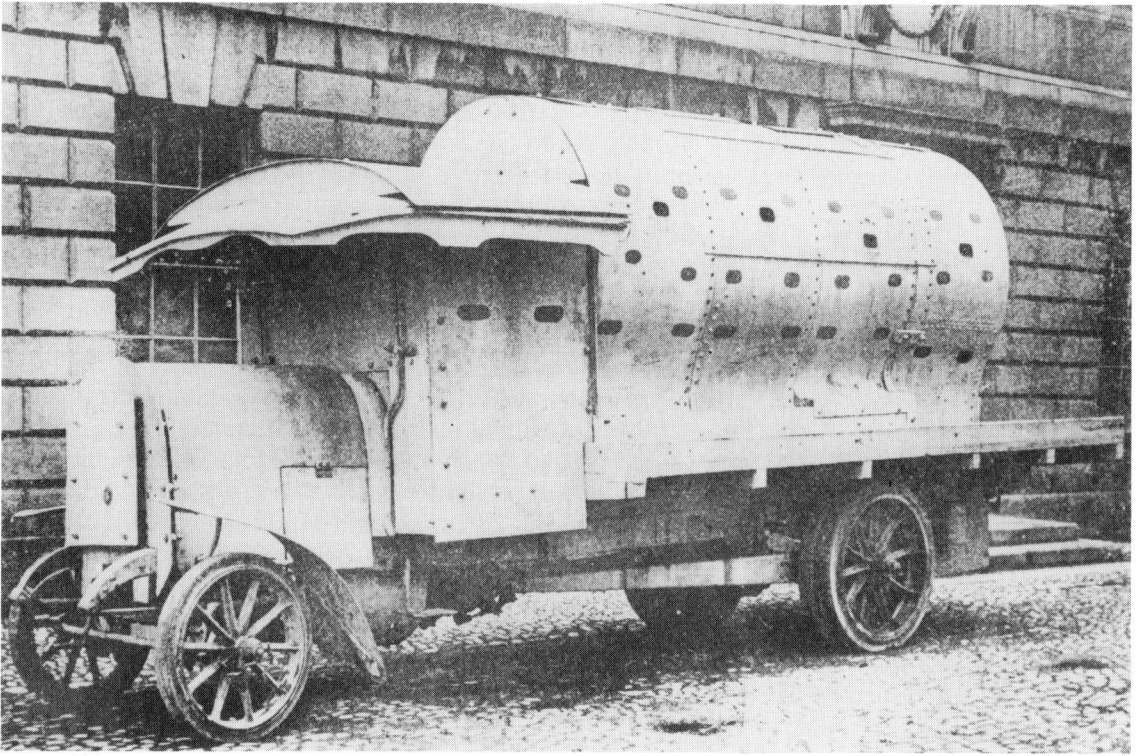

An armoured car in the front square of Trinity College, Dublin. It was made for the Lancers, British cavalrymen who became the first victims of the rebels occupying the GPO. This action demonstrated the ineffectiveness of horsemen as street-fighters against snipers in houses: hence the armoured car, which was hastily improvised from the boiler of a locomotive.

their lost opportunity than of having emerged successfully from their baptism of fire. Although the encounter with the Lancers was no more than a skirmish, its effect was to put new heart into the rebels. It was a victory, however small; and it demonstrated that military men could be just as incompetent as rank amateurs such as themselves. If the British persisted in such frontal assaults, whether they used cavalry or infantry units, the rebel forces would be able to inflict very heavy casualties on their enemies and put up a prolonged resistance. As the afternoon went on, despite the strain of waiting for a renewed British attack that never materialized, the men in the GPO remained in good spirits, especially after they received another item of encouraging news. Dublin Castle, the centre and symbol of the British administration in Ireland, had unexpectedly fallen to the rebels.

Rebels in action

College and castle

The party of rebels at the GPO was only one of several small contingents that had set off from Liberty Hall and other assembly points this Easter Monday morning. The main objective was to seize a ring of chosen sites, from the Four Courts in the west to Boland's Mills in the south-east of the city. These were so placed that forces controlling them could hope to contain attacks from the various British army barracks encircling Dublin, and to prevent reinforcements from England coming in by rail from Dublin's port, Kingstown (now Dun Laoghaire).

This did not alter the fact that the British already had two or three times as many men as the rebels in the city itself – or that the rebels' numbers were so small that they were unable to man certain vital points in the very heart of Dublin. One of these was Trinity College, the exclusively Protestant university whose students were mainly drawn from Ireland's pro-British upper class. Enclosed within high walls, the College offered excellent facilities for defence, and it is arguable that the rebels should have seized it despite the problem of patrolling so much territory. It could certainly have been taken at noon, and for some time afterwards, although students belonging to the University Officers' Training Corps did organize a defence of sorts, assisted by a few colonial soldiers whom they managed to bring in off the streets.

Another dauntingly large complex was Dublin Castle, whose thick walls enclosed two courtyards. It was a formidable obstacle for men without artillery, although in normal times it functioned as a palace rather than a fortress. "The Castle" was the administrative centre of British Ireland, and also its social centre, with a throne room and other splendid state apartments where the Lord Lieutenant or Viceroy – the nominal ruler of Ireland, representing the British King – presided over tea-parties, balls and presentations.

The rebels did make a demonstration against the Castle, though it was understandably half-hearted. At roughly the same time as James Connolly gave the order to charge the GPO, his namesake Sean Connolly led about a dozen Citizen

The United Kingdom and Eire, as partitioned in 1921

Dublin

Magazine Fort

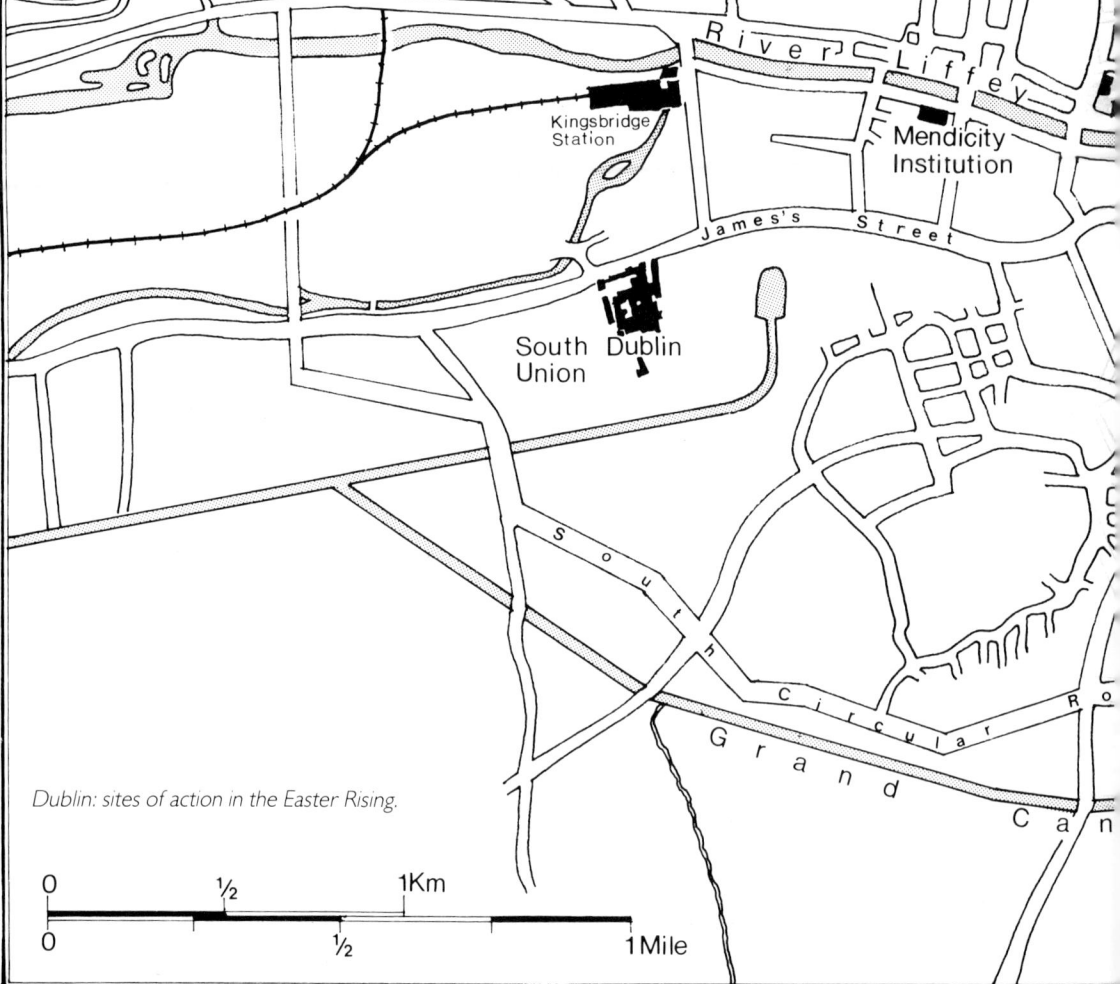

North Circular Road

River Liffey

Kingsbridge Station

Mendicity Institution

James's Street

South Dublin Union

South Circular Road

Grand Canal

Dublin: sites of action in the Easter Rising.

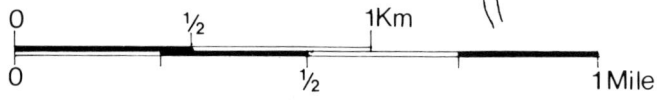

| 0 | ½ | 1Km |
| 0 | ½ | 1Mile |

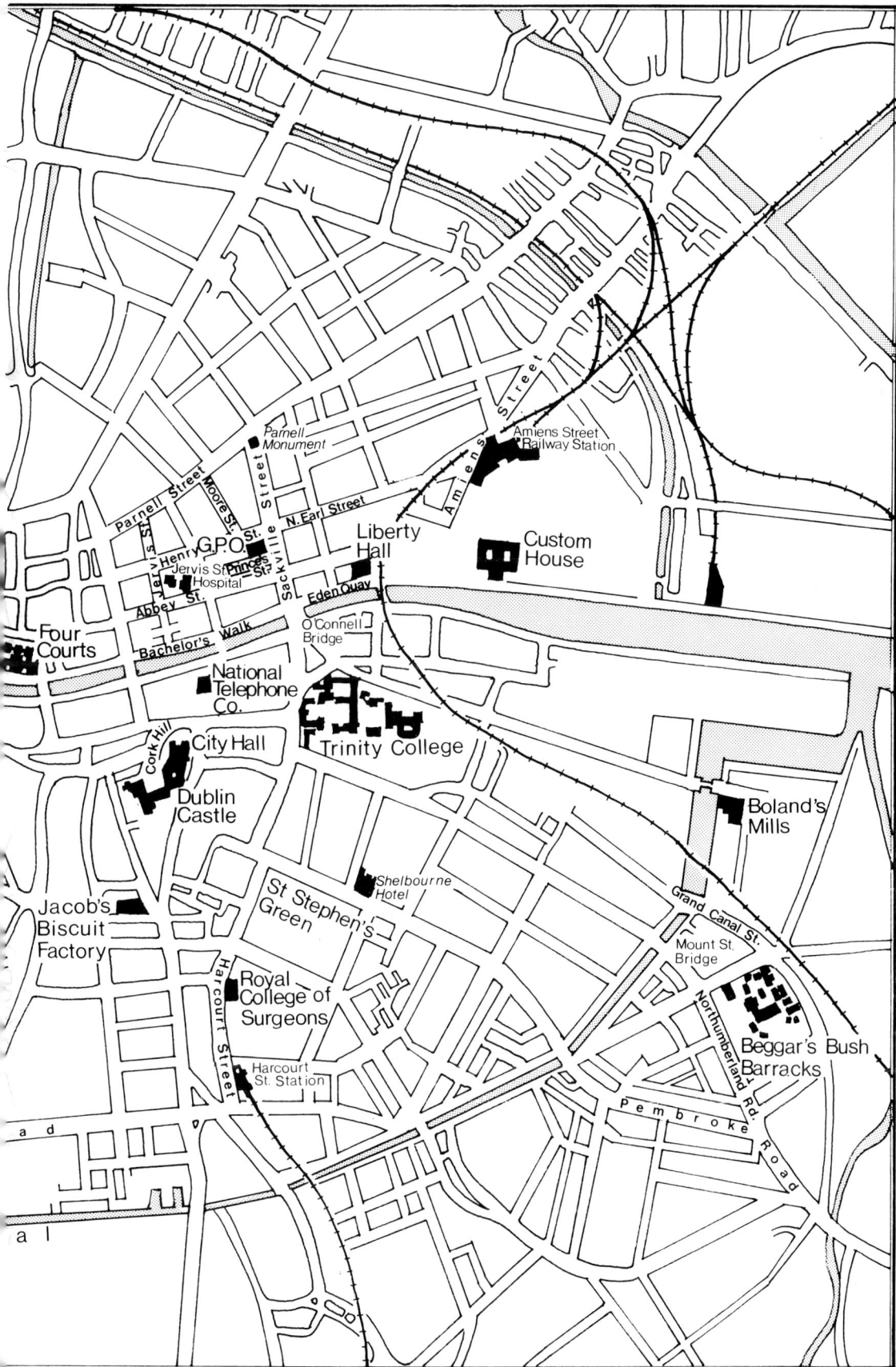

Parnell
Monument

Parnell Street

Moore St.

Amiens Street

Amiens Street
Railway Station

N. Earl Street

G.P.O.

Henry St.

Jervis St.
Hospital

Princes
St.

Sackville Street

Liberty
Hall

Custom
House

Abbey St.

Eden Quay

Bachelor's Walk

O'Connell
Bridge

Four
Courts

National
Telephone
Co.

Cork Hill

City Hall

Trinity College

Dublin
Castle

Boland's
Mills

Shelbourne
Hotel

St Stephen's
Green

Grand Canal St.

Jacob's
Biscuit
Factory

Harcourt Street

Royal
College of
Surgeons

Mount St.
Bridge

Northumberland Rd.

Beggar's Bush
Barracks

Harcourt
St. Station

Pembroke Road

a d

a l

A view of Dublin Castle, showing the state apartments. The Castle was the centre and symbol of British rule in Ireland.

Army men up Cork Hill to the front gate of the Castle. Their way was barred by a police constable and a soldier on sentry duty. Connolly shot the constable in the head, killing him almost instantaneously; this unlucky man was thus the first casualty of the rising. The sentry, whose rifle is said to have been loaded with blanks, beat a hasty retreat.

Unknown to the rebels, Dublin Castle was virtually undefended, although it was serving as a hospital for a large number of soldiers wounded in France. If they had marched boldly in, Connolly's troops might have captured the fortress, and with it the Irish Permanent Under-Secretary, Sir Matthew Nathan, who was the highest member of the British administration actually in the country at that time. This would certainly have been a propaganda coup, though it would not have changed the rebels' inability to man the Castle itself. Connolly may have been influenced by this consideration or, faced with an empty courtyard overlooked on all sides, he may have feared that he and his men were being lured into a trap. Whatever his reasons, after an exchange of shots he ordered his men to fall back. They occupied the adjacent City Hall (in effect Dublin's town hall) and other buildings from which they could pin down the Castle's defenders. Both sides were soon reinforced, and a sharpshooting match developed in which the rebels seem to have had rather the better of things. But Sean Connolly became the first rebel casualty of the rising when he was shot on the roof of City Hall by a British sniper.

The report received at the GPO, claiming that Dublin Castle had fallen, was simply wrong. One of the rebels' wives,

British soldiers in action against snipers during the Easter Rising. Irish sharpshooting was very effective in pinning down the enemy forces, and the rebels managed to hold out far longer than might have been expected.

despatched with a republican flag for the occupying force to raise above the captured Castle, soon discovered the true state of affairs and carried her disappointing news back to Sackville Street.

Raid on a fort

One dramatic little episode occurred well outside the centre of Dublin, at the Magazine Fort in the city's famous Phoenix Park. Although small, the fort was Dublin's most important munitions store, and as such was provided with defences that included a surrounding dry moat with only a single crossing-point. However, at Easter 1916 it was also undermanned and carelessly guarded, as the rebels knew. One of their number, Garry Holohan, had got a job with a firm employed to carry out repairs on the fort, and had mapped its layout and familiarized himself with the guards' routine. Armed with this information it might be possible for the rebels to seize the fort and gain possession of quantities of arms and explosives before signalling the rising to the world by blowing up the fort.

At about 12.15 p.m., when Patrick Daly and Holohan led a party of Volunteers against the fort, they had no difficulty in distracting and seizing the unsuspecting sentry at the gate. Once they were inside, only one man offered any resistance and was shot by Holohan. The rest of the garrison were rounded up and taken prisoner; Playfair, the commander of the fort, was away in France, but his wife and three children were among the captives.

The rebel plan had so far gone smoothly, but there was an unexpected hitch when it was discovered that the key to the main store had gone missing. The explanation was simple, if frustrating: the officer in charge had absent-mindedly put it in his pocket before going off to the Fairyhouse races! This was a piece of crass incompetence that might in some circumstances have proved disastrous for the British; but in the event it was a stroke of undeserved good luck. However, the rebels did find a relatively small cache of gelignite. Making the best of things, Patrick Daly ordered his men to stack it against the main store and light the fuses. The prisoners were set free; then the rebels, carrying off the few weapons they had captured, left the building and separated in order to join their units.

A few minutes later, the explosives store blew up with a disappointingly dull sound that was certainly not – as the rebels had hoped – heard all over Dublin. The entire incident is a good example of the way in which unforeseen factors so often control events: the raid on the fort, which was better planned and executed than most of the rebels' undertakings, failed to have the slightest effect on the course of the rising. Its sequel was a personal tragedy that underlined its futility. As he cycled away from the fort, Holohan spotted one of Mrs Playfair's boys running out of the park and up to the front door of a house; his mother had evidently sent him to let the authorities know what was happening. Rather than see him warn the British, Holohan cycled after the boy and shot him three times. It seems unlikely that the boy Playfair's message would have made much difference, since there were now other prisoners from the fort presumably making their way to telephones; and in any case the rising had already begun at other points in the city. Whether Holohan took a wise precaution or simply acted in a moment of panic, the boy lost his life.

Seizing strongpoints

The events at the GPO, Dublin Castle and the Magazine Fort showed that the British had been taken completely by surprise. Thanks to this factor, the rebels' operations went smoothly elsewhere in Dublin, despite the disappointingly low turnout of men prepared to fight. North of the river, a contingent led by Edmund Daly occupied the Four Courts, one of the many fine eighteenth-century buildings that gave Dublin its special atmosphere. Here the High Court sat and the barristers had their quiet chambers; but now quantities of the volumes of legal history and precedent lining the rooms were pulled down from the shelves and piled up to serve as sandbags. Across the Liffey, a short distance upriver, the Mendicity Institution was taken over by Sean Heuston and his men. A more important stronghold was the South Dublin Union off James's Street. This large, close-knit assemblage of poorhouse buildings offered good defensive prospects to a force of well-placed snipers. The occupying force was led by Eamonn Ceannt, one of the seven men who had formed the Provisional Government and signed the proclamation of a republic. Another signatory, the university lecturer and poet Thomas MacDonagh, took charge of an equally well-known Dublin landmark. This was Jacob's biscuit factory, a tall, triangular building from whose towers the rebels could keep Dublin Castle and the roads from the south under observation.

It was vital for the rebels to control the south-east approaches to the city, through which British reinforcements would come in by rail or road, across the Grand Canal. A detachment of Citizen Army men seized Harcourt Street railway station, while a larger contingent occupied an elegant little park, St Stephen's Green. Here the leaders were Michael Mallin, James Connolly's chief of staff and second-in-command, and Countess Markievicz. The countess was one of the most colourful figures in the rebel ranks, a tall, hawk-faced Irish aristocrat, born Constance Gore-Booth, who spoke with an upper-class English accent and had been presented at court. As a socialist organization, the Citizen Army recruited women as well as men, claiming that it offered both the chance to fight; and the countess, who was an excellent shot as well as a fiery, inspiring personality, held the rank of lieutenant. However, traditional attitudes towards women might have prevailed if the rising had been better supported. The countess's first task was to take medical

Thomas MacDonagh, who commanded the rebel forces controlling Jacob's factory.

supplies to Sean Connolly's men, whom she witnessed beginning their attack on Dublin Castle. Then she drove on to St Stephen's Green, where Mallin told her she must stay with him: he had only a few men, most of them untrained, and she must be prepared to fight as a sniper. First, however, Mallin left her in charge of the trench-digging and barricade-building in the Green while he supervised the construction of street-barricades. Some other Citizen Army girls had revolvers, with which they held up bread vans and obtained much-needed supplies of food. The countess herself took part in the requisitioning of vehicles, in one of which she found high-society acquaintances to whom, despite the exigencies of war, she apologized in her most gracious *grande dame* manner for the inconvenience she was causing. After a couple of hours Mallin promoted her to his official second-in-command

Countess Markievicz as a young woman. She is wearing the kind of formal dress in which she appeared at Dublin Castle and other places where vice-regal functions were held. Transformed into an ardent socialist and republican, she was to take an active part in the fighting during Easter Week, 1916.

and, as she later recalled in her cool, true-blue fashion, she discovered that "The work was very exciting when the fighting began. I continued round and round the Green, reporting back if anything was wanted, or tackling any sniper who was particularly objectionable."

The rifle shots at St Stephen's Green could be heard in the Boland's Mills area, where the 2nd battalion of Irish Volunteers had taken over Boland's Bakery. The man in command was Eamon de Valera, a little-known teacher of mathematics who had trained hard with the Volunteers and studied military manuals, but who had no practical experience of soldiering. Nevertheless he proved a capable, far-sighted leader. His task was to block the advance of the troops stationed at Beggar's Bush barracks, or of the anticipated British reinforcements arriving from Kingstown. Beggar's Bush gave the rebels no trouble: it was occupied by a handful of under-equipped soldiers who were only too thankful not to be attacked. But the threat of reinforcements from outside Dublin was a grave one: it meant that, in time, Boland's Bakery could be expected to face more British

Commandant Michael Mallin and Countess Markievicz, the leaders of the rebel forces at St Stephen's Green. Here they are under guard as British prisoners. Mallin was subsequently shot, but Countess Markievicz, sentenced to life imprisonment, was soon released, and in 1918 she became the first woman elected to the British parliament.

soldiers than any other rebel strongpoint. The position of the Bakery itself was ideal, overlooking the railway line and the bridge on Grand Canal Street. And to complete his defences de Valera positioned men at various key points along the Pembroke and Northumberland Roads, the other thoroughfares across the Grand Canal.

For most of the rebels, the early hours of the rising were a time of hard work rather than high excitement. Even at places where the shooting started almost at once, there were provisions to be laid in and barricades to be built with trams, cars and trash, as well as windows to be loopholed and sandbags to be heaved about; in some places, holes had to be knocked through the walls separating houses so that the rebels could cover long distances on a street without exposing themselves to enemy fire. Outside the strongpoints, snipers were distributed in nearby houses as widely as possible, often in ones and twos. This policy was dictated by shortage of manpower, but worked remarkably well, since an active sniper is harder to locate than a larger body of men, and can still pin down substantial numbers of the enemy; significantly, British reports consistently overestimated the numbers engaged on the rebels' side.

At this stage, however, it was not certain that the Easter Rising would last for more than a few hours. Faced with a mere 1600 men, surely the British would bring their overwhelming force to bear straight away, turning the rising into something worse than a failure: a fiasco.

Eamon de Valera, mathematics teacher and rebel commandant at Boland's Mills. In this photograph, taken after the end of the Easter Rising, he is a British prisoner, under sentence of death passed by a court-martial. However, de Valera survived to become the leading spokesman for the Irish nationalists in the United States. Although he led the losing side in the subsequent civil war, he was eventually to become prime minister and the foremost Irish statesman of his time.

Gathering storm

The British response

The events of Monday afternoon revealed some of the flaws in the rebels' planning. They had overlooked the importance of the telephone exchange, which remained in British hands; and although they disrupted telephone communications by cutting many of the wires, they failed to put them all out of action. At about 12.30, when the acting military governor of Ireland, Colonel Cowan, became aware that he was faced with an armed insurrection in Dublin, he was able to send out urgent calls for help. He managed to get through to the Curragh, the big military base in Kildare, which was ordered to despatch immediate reinforcements by train. Shortly afterwards an officer in mufti (civilian dress) cycled out to Kingstown, where the Admiralty wireless station cabled news of the rising to London. And only a little later the same day, Cowan arranged for more troops to be brought into Dublin from Belfast, Athlone and Tipperary.

Thanks to the rebels' success in achieving complete surprise, Cowan had no means of knowing how numerous they were. If he *had* known that the men under his immediate command outnumbered the rebels, it is arguable that the rising might have been nipped in the bud, or at any rate dealt with more rapidly and effectively than it was. Instead, Cowan played safe, moving slowly and taking few chances until he was certain that he had overwhelming force on his side. This was good military sense, but more dubious as a political policy, since it enabled Connolly and Pearse to achieve their minimum objective – to hold out long enough to make an impression on their fellow-Irishmen and the outside world. From the rebels' point of view, a swift fiasco – making their cause look ridiculous – would have been a worse outcome than a blood-bath.

As a result, the men in the GPO spent the first twenty-four hours of the rising waiting for an all-out onslaught that failed to materialize. However, although Cowan's information about the situation in Dublin was incomplete, he knew far more than the rebels did about what was happening in the rest of Ireland. In particular, he knew that there was little serious trouble outside the capital, and it was this fact that had allowed him to draft in such large numbers of troops by stripping the garrisons in the provinces. By contrast, Connolly and Pearse could only guess and hope, since the rebels' radio equipment was hopelessly inadequate. They could receive information (which might, however, be untrustworthy, reflecting distortion or censorship by the British), but they were unable to transmit anything. Attempts to remedy this with the help of equipment from the Marconi School, just across Sackville Street from the Post Office, proved unsuccessful, and so the republican cause remained unreported to the world – except by the British, who also controlled all the other media and were therefore able to ensure that their version of events was the one heard by most people.

Propaganda and "atrocities"

But for an unlucky, ludicrous accident, the world might have heard the rebels' side too. On the Friday before the rising, a party of five republicans had been sent down to Kerry, in the far south-west of Ireland. Their mission was to seize equipment from the government wireless station at Cahirciveen, then to reassemble it and use it to contact the expected German ship carrying arms for the rebels. In fact the ship was not there – it had arrived earlier, and had already been hunted down by the British and scuttled by its skipper – but the equipment would no doubt have found its way back to Dublin if the republican agents had ever reached the wireless station. They never did. Three of the five men went in a car whose driver lost his way, took the wrong turning at Killorglin, and drove to the end of the road at Ballykissane. Unfortunately, road's end was Ballykissane Quay on the River Laune. In the darkness the car went over into deep water, where the three agents drowned. If the rebel leaders did not hear the news from their own sources, they must have realized what had happened when they read of the mysterious Kerry drownings in the Monday newspapers.

The first public British reaction to the rising came during the afternoon and was, among other things, an act of propaganda. The Viceroy, Lord Wimborne, issued a proclamation:

"Whereas, an attempt, instigated and designed by the foreign enemies of our king and country to incite rebellion in Ireland, and thus endanger the safety of the United

Kingdom, has been made by a reckless, though small body of men, who have been guilty of insurrectionary acts in the city of Dublin:

Now we, Ivor Churchill, Baron Wimborne, Lord-Lieutenant-General and Governor-General of Ireland, do hereby warn all His Majesty's subjects that the sternest measures are being, and will be taken for the prompt suppression of the existing disturbances and the restoration of order."

And so on. Citizens were warned not to interfere with government actions, and cautioned against "unnecessarily" frequenting the streets or assembling in crowds; but martial law was not yet imposed. The interest of Wimborne's proclamation lay in its first sentence, which was to be echoed by most subsequent British propaganda. Like other occupying powers before and since, the British were to insist that a revolt against their benevolent rule could not possibly represent genuine native feeling, but must be inspired and paid for by foreign foes. In this instance, British prejudice cast Connolly and Pearse in the role of German agents, and later on their captors would be surprised to find that the Irishmen's pockets were *not* stuffed with Deutschmarks. Of course the rising was in no sense instigated by the Germans, though the rebels were, naturally enough, prepared to accept help from Germany – or any other power – if they could get it. It is hard to believe that men in authority such as Wimborne can have failed to realize this, although rage against "traitors" – meaning anyone whose loyalties differ from one's own – is highly infectious in wartime. But whether or not the "German agent" smear was consciously manipulated, it was widely believed outside Ireland.

British propaganda also made much of the "atrocities" perpetrated by the rebels. The worst of these occurred late on Monday afternoon, when a detachment of the Irish Volunteer Defence Corps came marching up Northumberland Road. This body had no connection with the nationalist Irish Volunteers, and enjoyed official approval. Though khaki-clad, its members were not regular soldiers but middle-aged Irish reservists, roughly comparable to a Home Guard ("Dad's Army"). Dubliners regarded them with tolerant amusement, and since their uniforms carried the royal initials GR (Georgius Rex – King George), labelled them "Gorgeous Wrecks" or "God's Rejected". On this occasion the reservists had been on a route march and were carrying rifles, although these were not in fact loaded. When they came in sight, the rebels stationed at Boland's Mills took them for British soldiers and opened fire, with devastating effect: five Gorgeous Wrecks were killed and nine wounded before de Valera's men realized their mistake. Although it was represented as a "massacre", the shooting was clearly an accident of the kind that inevitably occurs in civil or guerrilla warfare. If anyone is to blame in such situations, it is – depending on your political sympathies – those who start a rising or civil war, or those whose policy of domination makes risings and wars the only means of securing freedom.

The most sustained actions on Monday afternoon took place around Dublin Castle and at the South Dublin Union. Ceannt's small band of men could not hope to hold the huge area of the Union by conventional defence, and gradually retreated when fifty British soldiers entered the grounds. However, the rebels' guerrilla tactics were so effective, and the sheer size of the Union provided them with so many strongpoints and concealed places, that they were able to put up a highly effective resistance. At the Castle, the British defences were reinforced by about 2 p.m. when 180 men of the Royal Irish Rifles and the Royal Dublin Fusiliers made their way into the building from Ship Street. The balance tilted further in the late afternoon, when troop-trains began to arrive from the Curragh at Kingsbridge Station, which lay between the South Dublin Union and the right bank of the Liffey. Here too the rebels were handicapped by their small numbers; with a larger force, Ceannt might have seized and held the station, whereas the few snipers within range could not prevent mass disembarkations of men and materials. By about 6 p.m. a substantial body of fresh troops had worked their way round to Ship Street, relieved the Castle, and prepared to take the offensive.

Eamonn Ceannt in 1915. As commandant at the South Dublin Union, Ceannt held out against overwhelming odds until the final rebel surrender.

Shooters and looters

Communications between the GPO and the other strongpoints were still good, and Connolly was kept informed of events – and also of non-events such as the capture of the Castle, now known to be a baseless rumour. The rebels were still busy in and around Sackville Street, barricading Earl Street against the expected attack from the east and evacuating Liberty Hall. As word of the rising spread, girls of the Cumann na mBan and small numbers of Irish Volunteers trickled into the Post Office; some of the girls were allowed to stay on as cooks and nurses, but most of the men were sent out in small groups to reinforce the rebel positions in other parts of Dublin.

Something of a holiday atmosphere prevailed in Sackville Street, and for a time discipline was so lax that sightseers were tolerated on the roof of the GPO. However, it gradually became apparent that any difficulties that occurred in the next few hours were more likely to be caused by rampaging Dubliners than by British soldiers. At about three o'clock women began queuing outside the Post Office, expecting to be paid their "separation money". This was a small allowance made by the British government to mothers and wives of soldiers fighting in France; there were many thousands of Irishmen in the British army, and to the women left behind in the dreadful slums of Dublin, separation money was a vital supplementary income. Those who queued outside the Post Office were understandably enraged to learn that the new Irish government had no intention of honouring British commitments, and a near-riot ensued.

Rebel barricade at the south-west corner of St Stephen's Green. It consisted mainly of commandeered motor cars.

Meanwhile, the crowds had returned to Sackville Street after the retreat of the Lancers. Whereas many of the earlier onlookers had been holidaymaking members of the middle class, the majority now were slum-dwellers who relished the absence of the police and increasingly felt in the mood to take advantage of it. By accident or intention, the window of Noblett's sweet shop, just across Sackville Street from the GPO, was suddenly shattered. People eagerly climbed in to take what they could, and their example set off an orgy of looting. The high-minded rebels in the GPO – forbidden by their leaders even to sample an alcoholic drink – were horrified by the behaviour of their fellow-countrymen, who were undeterred by shots fired over their heads and ignored the pleas and commands of priests who tried to intervene. When Sean T. O'Kelly reported that he had failed to drive back the crowd, Connolly told him that he should have quelled them by shooting a few of the looters. But although he may have thought such an action justified in theory, Connolly could not bring himself to order it. After all, these were the people for whom he, as a socialist revolutionary and nationalist, was going into battle; and he knew enough of their deprivations to understand their snatching at the good things of life when there was no one to stop them. All the same, the looting was the sort of incident that might be used to discredit the rising, and did nothing to raise the morale of

Dublin's slums were among the worst in Europe. Ironically, the coming of the First World War improved the lot of the Dublin poor, many of whom were therefore hostile to the rebels. However, slum-dwellers did take advantage of the collapse of law and order during the rising, and there was looting on a large scale.

the men in the Post Office, tensely waiting for the British onslaught.

At about 9.30 p.m., some children playing with stolen fireworks set fire to the Cable Boot Shop, next to the Imperial Hotel. The Dublin fire service was still functioning, but by the time the blaze was under control a new fire had started elsewhere. The destruction of Sackville Street had begun even before the British attacked.

Inside the Post Office, as it got later, one of the busiest people was the apparently incongruous figure of Father John Flanagan. He was there because Patrick Pearse, scrupulously pious, had been anxious for the spiritual welfare of his men, not all of whom had recently received the sacrament or confessed, despite the strong possibility that they would be dead the following day. Rather than let them go into action with their sins upon them, Pearse had persuaded Father Flanagan, who was a curate at the nearby Pro-Cathedral, to come to the Post Office, where he heard one confession after another until 11.30 that night.

One last decision was taken before the rebels' day ended. At ten o'clock, Sean MacDermott emerged from a heated confrontation with The O'Rahilly, and ordered Sean T. O'Kelly to proceed to a private house in the northern suburb of Cabra Park, where he was to deliver an order for the release of a well-known Irish Volunteer leader named Bulmer Hobson. Like The O'Rahilly, Hobson belonged to the faction within the Volunteers that had opposed the rising; and MacDermott had been sufficiently fearful of his influence to arrange for him to be kidnapped on Good Friday night. On Easter Monday night in the GPO, The O'Rahilly demanded and obtained Hobson's release; there was, in any case, no reason to hold him once the fighting had started. O'Kelly executed his mission without difficulty, although plenty of shots were still being exchanged late into the night. Hobson was freed, but unlike The O'Rahilly he was not tempted to join the insurrection. He went quietly home.

O'Kelly's night was not over yet. He delivered a letter from Tom Clarke to his wife; she took the opportunity to ask after her brother, Edmund Daly, who was in command at the Four Courts. Then O'Kelly visited his own mother before making his way back to the Post Office. At about 2 a.m., after a remarkably hectic day, he made up a bed under the front counter in the main hall, using mailbags for his pillow and mattress. Then he pulled some blankets over him, and went to sleep.

The fate of the rising

Events on the day following the rising were deceptively undramatic, though the situation was gradually changing even in the small hours of Tuesday morning. Special trains brought many more British troops into Kingsbridge Station, and a senior officer, Brigadier-General W.H.M. Lowe, arrived to take charge of operations. Still uncertain of the rebels' strength, he devised a plan to reduce the city slowly and methodically rather than by swift and spectacular action. The main British effort would be devoted to consolidating their hold on the area around Dublin Castle and Trinity College, from which a wedge could be driven through the enemy positions along the line of the River Liffey. With the GPO and the Four Courts isolated from the rebel outposts south of the river, the republican strongholds could be destroyed one by one.

One place where the British did seize the initiative at once was St Stephen's Green. At about 4 a.m. 120 British troops occupied the Shelburne Hotel and set up machine guns on the upper floors. Since the hotel was the tallest of the buildings overlooking the square, the rebels' failure to seize it was a serious – and almost incomprehensible – mistake. The trenches they had dug, presumably in imitation of the trenches on the Western Front, were of little value – pointless if the buildings surrounding the square were also in rebel hands, and indefensible if they were not. By daybreak British fire had driven the rebels from their trenches and into the Royal College of Surgeons on Harcourt Street, just below the Green. However, despite their tactical blunders, the rebels under Mallin and Markievicz now started to put up a stiff resistance.

At the Post Office, all attempts to mend the radio equipment from the Marconi School had failed. But although no certain news was to be had from the rest of Ireland, there was a growing conviction that this could mean only one thing – that the country had remained quiet. (With a handful of minor exceptions, this proved to be the case.) In Dublin itself it was still fairly easy to move about north of the river by avoiding the main streets barricaded by the British, and on Tuesday morning supplies of ammunition continued to be brought into the Post Office from secret dumps in the city. However, in some places it was only possible to smuggle things past the British by concealing them under the dresses of the Cumann na mBan girls; and when Connolly sent out a contingent of men to cross the river and reinforce City Hall, which was now under great pressure, they were unable to get through. The British were in fact clearing the Castle area, according to plan, capturing City Hall, the *Express* and *Evening Mail* buildings and other points, though their bayonet charges and room-by-room searches cost them many casualties. Soon they were able to seal off this sector completely, occupying the streets below the O'Connell Bridge, although they did not as yet risk crossing the bridge itself.

Irish War News

At noon, exactly twenty-four hours after the beginning of the Easter Rising, the rebels published their own newspaper, *Irish War News*, which was subtitled "The Irish Republic" and priced one penny. It was a curious production, since the first three of its four pages carried no mention of the rising, but contained argumentative essays of the sort that might have appeared in any republican news-sheet in ordinary times. A reader who failed to notice the subtitle might well have given up at page three and thrown away what is now seen as a historic document! The real news was given in just over a column on the back page, under the heading STOP PRESS! THE IRISH REPUBLIC. After announcing the declaration of a republic and listing the members of its Provisional Government, *Irish War News* quoted the text of a statement that Pearse had written earlier that morning:

"The Irish Republic was proclaimed in Dublin on Easter Monday, 24th April, at 12 noon. Simultaneously with the issue of the proclamation of the Provisional Government the Dublin Division of the Army of the Republic, including the Irish Volunteers, Citizen Army, Hibernian Rifles, and other bodies, occupied dominating points in the city. The G.P.O. was seized at 12 noon, the Castle was attacked at the same moment, and shortly afterwards the Four Courts were occupied. The Irish troops hold the City Hall and dominate the Castle. Attacks were immediately commenced by the British forces and were everywhere

37

repulsed. At the moment of writing this report, (9.30 a.m., Tuesday) the Republican forces hold all their positions and the British forces have nowhere broken through. There has been heavy and continuous fighting for nearly 24 hours, the casualties of the enemy being much more numerous than those on the Republican side. The Republican forces everywhere are fighting with splendid gallantry. The populace of Dublin are plainly with the Republic, and the officers and men are everywhere cheered as they march through the streets. The whole centre of the city is in the hands of the Republic, whose flag flies from the G.P.O."

Pearse went on to claim that "Communication with the country is largely cut, but reports to hand show that the country is rising, and bodies of men from Kildare and Fingall have already reported in Dublin." Communiqués issued in wartime are designed to reassure the combatants on one side and win the sympathy of the uncommitted; they are propaganda, and as such aim to be plausible but not uncomfortably true; and Pearse's description of the situation was no exception to this rule.

Aftermath: in the British vice

By this time Pearse must have been certain that the insurrection was doomed, though he told one of his men – and may even have believed – that German U-boats had been sighted in Dublin Bay; even this kind of help could not have done more than prolong the agony. By Tuesday afternoon British forces were already pushing back the rebels in the north-west and north-east of the city, using artillery to break up their barricades.

According to legend (and it may be no more than that), James Connolly assured his followers that the British would never use artillery in Dublin; as a socialist, he is supposed to have believed that a "bourgeois" government, which existed to protect private property, would never willingly cause millions of pounds' worth of damage. If that was really what Connolly thought, he was utterly mistaken. On Wednesday morning the gunboat *Helga* sailed up the Liffey and began to bombard Liberty Hall (which, though the British did not know it, had already been evacuated). This proved to be the preliminary to a sustained artillery assault that began in the afternoon and, over the next few days, reduced Sackville Street and the area around it to rubble and ruins.

Sackville Street and Eden Quay after the British bombardment.

As the British grip tightened, the rebels fell back to their strongpoints, and took on the character of isolated garrisons under siege. But inside these they held out with remarkable determination. The Mendicity Institution, which Heuston had been instructed to hold for a few hours, was only evacuated after three days. And except for the GPO, all the other strongpoints – the Four Courts, the South Dublin Union, Jacob's biscuit factory, the College of Surgeons and Boland's Mills – were still in action, and willing to fight on, when the end came. The rebels' most spectacular military success was in fact achieved by a handful of men in the Boland's Mills area who held up several companies of Sherwood Foresters for two days, preventing them from crossing the Mount Street Bridge into the city. Stationed in well-chosen vantage points overlooking the streets, the rebels, commanded by Captain Michael Malone, inflicted almost half the casualties suffered by the British during the entire period of the rising. They were only overwhelmed on the Friday by sheer weight of numbers; most of them, including Malone, died fighting.

However, it gradually became apparent that the main British target was the Post Office, now certainly identified as the rebel headquarters. Shells rained down on Sackville Street, but although many buildings were destroyed, British marksmanship was not accurate enough to do more than superficial damage to the GPO. On Thursday, in the face of the slow British advance, Connolly led out a party to try to construct a new barricade, when a spent bullet ricocheted and smashed his ankle. He was rescued from the street and treated by a captured British army doctor, but for long

39

periods he was in terrible pain and could no longer direct operations.

Meanwhile, raging fires and British pressure drove the surviving rebels from the east side of Sackville Street. Soon the entire force – some 300 men and women – was concentrated in the GPO. Attempts to dig a tunnel to safety proved impractical, and the rebel leaders realized that they could not hope to hold out for much longer. However, Pearse declared himself satisfied with what they had achieved. Recalling a famous rebellion of earlier times, Pearse told a former pupil, "Emmet's insurrection was nothing compared to this, you know. They will talk of Dublin in the future as one of the splendid cities, as they speak today of Paris. Dublin's name will be glorious forever."

British soldiers inside the General Post Office. Although several times hit by shells, and gutted by fire, the GPO survived the Easter Rising. It remains one of Dublin's historic sites.

The surrender

On Friday, 28th April, fires caused by incendiary bombs in the GPO itself blazed up out of control, and one floor after another had to be abandoned. At noon, most of the women in the building were evacuated under a Red Cross flag.

Tom Clarke (above) was among the defenders at the Post Office, although he was past military age and greatly enfeebled by the fifteen years he had spent in English gaols. However, as the representative of the nineteenth-century "Fenian" revolutionary tradition, he was revered by younger men such as his protégé, Sean MacDermott (above right), who was also known by the Gaelic version of his name, MacDiarmada. Both men were members of the Provisional Government set up by the rebels, and were consequently executed by the British after the failure of the rising.

Gunpowder, gelignite and food stores were moved down to the basement, but fires soon broke out there too, threatening to end the siege in a single moment by touching off the explosives.

The rebels' only remaining chance was to break through the British lines. The O'Rahilly led thirty men in a forlorn attack on the enemy barricade at the top of Moore Street, hoping against hope to fight his way through to a soap factory on Parnell Street which might serve as a new republican strongpoint. But the barricade was strongly manned, and most of the rebels, including The O'Rahilly, were shot down. Nonetheless, the evacuation of the GPO went forward. The prisoners were turned loose, and the rebels – led by Pearse with drawn sword, accompanied by Connolly, carried on a stretcher – dashed across Henry Street. Although they scattered under a hail of British bullets, most of them found their way to a little house close to Moore Street, where they spent the night. A few hours later, the building reverberated with the shock of the exploding gunpowder and gelignite, which had finally gone off in the GPO.

On Saturday morning the rebels established themselves in a row of houses on Moore Street, remaining under cover by knocking holes in the walls separating one dwelling from its neighbour. But at a council of war held just after noon, they recognized the hopelessness of their situation. Moore Street lay right under the British guns, which would have no trouble in smashing a rather ordinary row of shops and houses; and these were full not only of rebels but of large families which, having nowhere to go, had not taken the advice to evacuate given by the new British commander, General Sir John Maxwell, who had declared his determination to bombard any building harbouring rebels.

In view of these facts, the rebels took the decision to

The surrender document, signed by Patrick Pearse and counter-signed by James Connolly and Thomas MacDonagh on 29th April, 1916. Many rebels at Boland's Mills and elsewhere wanted to fight on, and were only persuaded with difficulty to obey Pearse's order.

In order to prevent the further slaughter of Dublin citizens, and in the hope of saving the lives of our followers now surrounded and hopelessly outnumbered, the members of the Provisional Government present at Head-Quarters have agreed to an unconditional surrender, and the Commandants of the various districts in the City and Country will order their commands to lay down arms.

P. H. Pearse
29th April 1916
3.45 p.m.

I agree to these conditions for the men only under my own Command in the Moore Street District and for the men in the Stephen's Green Command.

James Connolly
April 29/16

On consultation with Commandant Ceannt and other officers I have decided to agree to unconditional surrender also

Thomas MacDonagh.

Patrick Pearse formally surrenders to Brigadier-General Lowe on behalf of the republican forces.

surrender. A Cumann na mBan nurse, Elizabeth O'Farrell, emerged from Moore Street with a white flag, and after various adventures returned with a note from Brigadier-General Lowe. There was no offer to negotiate terms: Lowe would accept nothing but an unconditional surrender. Pearse had no choice but to agree, and handed over his sword to Lowe at 2.30 p.m. The other centres of rebel resistance were ordered to lay down their arms; they obeyed, though in some instances only after a certain amount of argument. As Pearse was driven away into captivity, a British officer – taken in by his own side's propaganda – remarked, "It would be interesting to know how many Marks [i.e. how much German money] that fellow has in his pocket."

The following day, marching through the city on their way to internment, the rebels found most Dubliners silently hostile; and in some streets they were pelted with rotten fruit by vociferous slum-dwellers waving union jacks. Three days later the courts-martial and the executions began. To all appearances the rising had ended in utter failure.

THE
INVESTIGATION

What caused "the Irish problem"?

Whose problem? A simple answer to "What caused 'the Irish problem'?" might be: the English. Englishmen have spoken for centuries of an "Irish problem", but an Irishman might with equal justice call it "the English problem". For the occupying power, all the difficulties were caused by the seeming impossibility of thoroughly subjugating or Anglicizing the natives; whereas from an Irish point of view the difficulties stemmed from the apparently overwhelming and immovable nature of English (and later British) power.

Geography and politics The surprising feature of the problem is not that it arose, but that it remained unresolved over several centuries. After all, it was natural enough in power-political terms that the larger and more populous island should seek political and economic domination of its smaller, weaker neighbour. And since the British Isles constitute a geographical unit, complete political unification could be expected to be the eventual outcome, and one that would in the long run be of mutual advantage to both islands. Yet, time and again, differences of culture, social system and religion – and perhaps a few lucky or unlucky accidents – prevented this fusion, and ultimately brought about a complete separation.

The "Norman Conquest" The English presence in Ireland dated from 1167, when English nobles and their followers were called in to help one side during an Irish civil war. These "English" mercenaries were in reality Normans, descended from the conquerors of Anglo-Saxon England in 1066 and not yet wholly assimilated; sometimes their half-and-halfness is indicated by describing them as Anglo-Normans. Thanks to their military superiority, they soon became an independent force in possession of large Irish holdings. To the King of England, Henry II, they posed a potential threat which he tried to head off by an expedition to Ireland in 1171. Backed by a papal grant (issued by Hadrian IV, the only English pope), Henry successfully asserted his claim to be the rightful king of Ireland.

Medieval Ireland   The Norman conquest of Ireland brought two very different cultures face to face. The native Irish spoke Gaelic, whereas the newcomers' language was Norman French, which in later centuries gradually gave way to English. Irish society was organized on a tribal basis; it consisted of separate clans, made up from family groupings, and functioned through communal decision-making and largely communal ownership of land. By contrast, the Anglo-Normans introduced the feudal system, based on private ownership and strictly defined legal and military obligations. Despite the distinguished history of Gaelic culture, the Normans regarded the native Irish as barbarians, yet there was a persistent tendency for each wave of settlers to "go native" after a generation or two – so much so that, as early as 1367, they were being forbidden by law to adopt Irish customs or speak in Gaelic. However, for most of the Middle Ages the English king's grip on Ireland was very loose, and even at the end of the fifteenth century his writ did not run very far outside the Dublin area.

The Elizabethan   Real control of Ireland by the English dates from the reign of
conquest   Queen Elizabeth (1588-1603). By this time, Anglo-Irish conflict had taken on a religious dimension, since England was now officially Protestant, whereas the overwhelming majority of Irishmen had remained true to the "Old Faith", Catholicism, and continued to acknowledge the Pope as the head of the Christian Church. In an age of extreme mutual intolerance, this meant that war and domination became still more self-righteously bloody and ruthless. The English war effort was exhausting and expensive, and the last leader of Irish resistance, the Earl of Tyrone, only capitulated at the very end of Elizabeth's reign. The help that Tyrone had received from England's Spanish enemies convinced subsequent English rulers that it was essential to control "England's back door", though of course the rigours of English rule equally convinced the Irish that they must look to England's enemies – first France, later Germany – for assistance in throwing off the alien yoke.

At one Mr. Atkins house 7 Papistes brake in & beate out his braines. then riped upe his Wife with Childe after they had rauished her. & Nero like vewed natures bed of conception then tooke they the Childe and sacrificed it in the fire

English Protestantes striped naked & turned into the mountaines in the frost, & snowe, whereof many hundreds are perished to death, & many lyinge deadl in diches & Sauages upbraided them saynge, now are ye wilde Irish as well as wee.

A Protestant account of Catholic atrocities, said to have been perpetrated during the great revolt of the 1640s. The harshness of the English and Protestant regime certainly provoked savage reprisals during the revolt, which was prolonged by the civil war between King and Parliament that convulsed England during this period. The Catholics were in their turn treated with savagery when England's new "strong man", Oliver Cromwell, landed in Ireland and crushed the revolt.

Plantations and confiscations

Tyrone's power-base had been the wild northern province of Ulster. Elizabeth's successor, James I, was persuaded to tame the province once and for all by expelling the native Irish and granting lands on favourable terms to Protestant English and Scottish settlers. (When James, already King of Scotland as James VI, inherited the English throne in 1603, the two countries were united – informally at first – as Great Britain.) The operation was a success – from a British point of view – and from this time onwards the government in London could rely on a large, loyal Protestant bloc in the North of Ireland. After a serious Catholic revolt in the 1640s, which was brutally suppressed by Oliver Cromwell, the policy of

The battle of the Boyne (1690) was a relatively small-scale encounter, but the victory of Britain's new king, William III (William of Orange), discouraged the deposed James II, who abandoned his Catholic supporters to their fates. As a result, Ireland was destined to remain under Protestant and English control for another two centuries.

confiscations was extended, largely wiping out the Catholics as a landowning class.

The Orangemen's hour

Catholic hopes of better times rose high when James II, a Catholic convert, became king. But James's policies alienated the Protestant establishment in England, and he soon lost his throne to his Protestant daughter Mary and her Dutch husband, William of Orange, who became King William III. Catholic Ireland rose to support James, who landed at Kinsale in March 1687, hoping to recover at least part of his former dominions. For a time the Irish Protestants seemed in grave danger, but the besieged Ulstermen held out heroically at Londonderry, and in July 1690 William of Orange defeated James at the battle of the Boyne. These two events were (and are) celebrated every year by the "Orangemen", as Irish Protestants who kept up the old antagonisms were to be called. Londonderry and the Boyne gave Orangemen a strong sense of separate identity – and a feeling of being permanently under threat from the Catholic majority – that influence events in Ireland to this day.

The penal code

James left Ireland after the battle of the Boyne, but his supporters struggled on and, after withstanding a siege at Limerick, secured honourable terms from King William's commanders. All Irish soldiers who wished to do so were allowed to take ship for France, in whose service the Irish Brigade was to distinguish itself on many occasions. The other terms, including religious liberty, were shamelessly violated: the English parliament ratified the agreement, but it was rejected by the Irish legislature – which was wholly Protestant – and no English authority cared to insist. In fact, shaken by the near-success of the Catholics in the war, the Irish parliament went on to enact a penal code that has been plausibly compared with the Nazi treatment of "inferior" peoples such as the Poles. Among other things, Catholics were not allowed to vote, to hold any public office, to work as civil servants, to practise law, to teach, or to print or sell books; and other measures were designed to ensure that Catholic estates and businesses remained small. As far as possible, then, Catholics were to be kept in serf-like poverty and ignorance. For public purposes, "Ireland" meant the concentrated Protestant minority in the North and a thinly spread Protestant landowning class that controlled the rest of Ireland. This last group, the Anglo-Irish or "Ascendancy", was the more important because its members were aristocrats or gentlefolk, and belonged to the Church of Ireland – the Established Church (equivalent to the Church of England) for whose upkeep all Irishmen were compelled to pay. The Ascendancy evolved a gracious, cultivated way of life that produced many outstanding men from Jonathan Swift, the author of *Gulliver's Travels*, to the playwright Oscar Wilde; but such grace and cultivation were supported by the toil of exploited Catholic labourers and tenant farmers. Many Irish landlords were absentees whose bailiffs were instructed to squeeze every penny from their estates, and the Irish property laws degraded the tenant farmer in particular, allowing him no security of tenure and positively encouraging the landlord to evict him if he increased the value of his smallholding by making improvements.

Irishmen united? In the course of time, some Protestants began to sympathize with the Catholics' plight, and a Protestant Irish nationalism developed as it became apparent that Britain controlled the island for her own economic benefit and against the interests of most Irishmen of all çreeds. Some of the greatest Irish national leaders, including Swift, Wolfe Tone and Parnell, were of Protestant stock. Tone and his followers, inspired by the libertarian ideas of the French Revolution, founded the Society of United Irishmen, open to Catholics and Protestants alike. But their insurrection was suppressed, and the only immediate result was the Act of Union (1801) whereby a bribed Irish parliament voted itself out of existence and made Ireland an integral part of Great Britain, sending MPs to the parliament at Westminster.

Catholic Emancipation The reforming spirit of the nineteenth century swept away many abuses. It was generally opposed to religious intolerance, although anti-"papist" feeling ran strong enough to cause a serious political crisis at Westminster before Catholic Emancipation (1829) gave the Catholics of Great Britain the same civil rights as their fellow-citizens. A leading part in the struggle for Catholic Emancipation was played by the Irish politician Daniel O'Connell, "the Liberator", after whom Dublin's main street is named; formally speaking, it was already O'Connell Street in 1916, but in those days most Dubliners still called it Sackville Street, which is why that name is used in the "Events" section of this book.

The Famine and the Fenians Disaster struck Ireland in 1846-49, when the potato crop failed. In large part because of the economic oppression

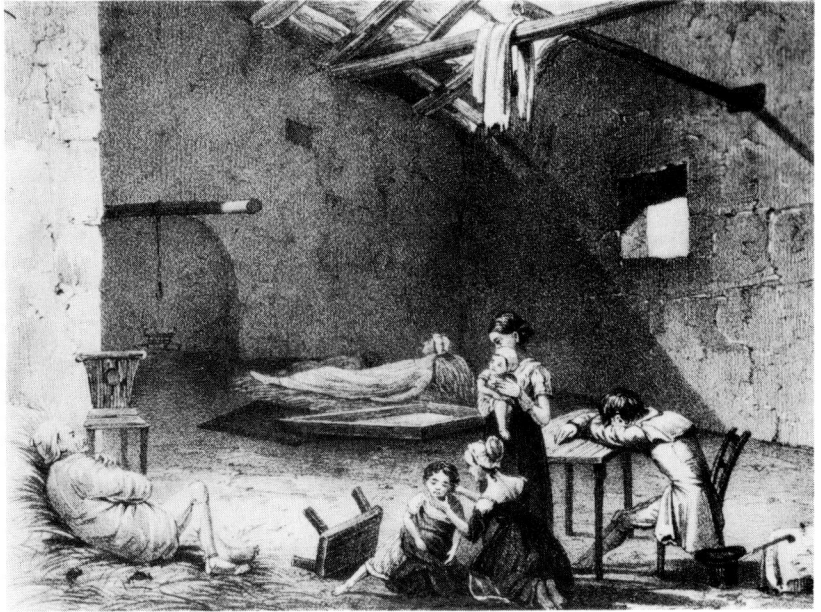

Famine in Ireland. This print, though sympathetically intended, hardly captures the misery and starvation that resulted from the failure of the potato crop in 1846 and subsequent years. At least a million Irish people died and another million and a half emigrated. From this point the population declined steadily for almost a century.

practised by landlords, Ireland had developed a one-crop agriculture, and the potato blight meant widespread starvation. More than a million people died in the Irish Famine, and between 1846 and 1855 some 1,500,000 emigrated, mainly to the United States, where they ultimately formed a large, prosperous and influential pressure group. The flood of emigration continued even when the direct effects of the Famine had ended: Ireland became a country which the young and active left as soon as they could, and this trend lasted for well over a hundred years. Anti-British agitation intensified with the foundation of the Irish Republican Brotherhood (IRB), a secret society of dedicated revolutionaries, and, in the USA, the Fenian Brotherhood;

Fenian revolutionaries on trial. The secret society of Fenians was the nineteenth-century forerunner of the Irish Republican Brotherhood, which initiated the Easter Rising.

both bodies, and Irish revolutionaries in general, tended to be labelled "Fenians" during the late nineteenth century.

Parnell and parliamentarianism

The Fenian rising of 1867 was a failure, and it began to seem increasingly likely that Ireland's wrongs could be righted by less violent means. The Liberal Party, led by Gladstone ("My mission is to pacify Ireland"), took a sympathetic line which also came to seem politically shrewd as a strong, united Irish Party emerged in the House of Commons. The party – eventually known as the Irish Nationalist Party – was organized and led by Charles Stewart Parnell. On occasion this bloc of Irish MPs held the balance between the Conservative and Liberal parties, and could therefore exact concessions in return for their support. Additional pressure was exerted by the Irish peasantry, whose boycotts and "no rent" campaigns made life difficult for the landlord class. As a result, by the early 1900s, the Church of Ireland had been disestablished (that is, shorn of its official, privileged status) and the position of the Irish peasantry had been improved beyond recognition. But Parnell's ultimate goal, Home Rule (that is, a self-governing Ireland not necessarily fully independent of Britain), was not achieved. Home Rule Bills were twice passed by the British House of Commons, in 1886 and 1893, only to be vetoed by the House of Lords, in which there was a permanent and overwhelming Conservative majority. The Home Rule movement was also weakened by the fall of Parnell (1890), who lost the leadership of his party when a Conservative Party intrigue made public his connection with Mrs Kitty O'Shea who, though long separated from her husband, was nonetheless a married woman. In Victorian terms this was a scandalous situation that no public man's career could hope to survive.

Home Rule in sight

After a long period of Conservative rule, the Liberals returned to power in 1906. When they came into conflict with the House of Lords, they bought Irish Nationalist support with the promise of Home Rule. As a result, the Liberals won the struggle, and the Parliament Act of 1911 broke the power of the Lords. This also removed the last obstacle to Home Rule. Despite fierce opposition from the Conservatives, the Protestant Ulstermen and some military circles, a Home Rule Act finally became law in September 1914. Ireland would become self-governing, and with the disappearance of her grievances she would become a loyal member of the British Empire. The "Irish problem" appeared to have been solved at last.

Why did the rising take place?

Doubts and suspicions   Superficially, the granting of Home Rule in 1914 seemed to vindicate the peaceful, parliamentarian strategy of the Irish Nationalist Party, now led by John Redmond. However, Irish doubts about British intentions persisted, since the Home Rule measures were immediately suspended because of the European war that had broken out in the previous month. Confidence was also undermined by the crises and uncertainties that accompanied the entire Home Rule controversy in 1911-14; they convinced many impatient and politically conscious Irishmen that the British government was either insincere or simply lacking in the will to carry out its policy in the face of determined opposition.

"The Orange card"   The fiercest opposition to Home Rule came from the Protestants of Ulster, who kept alive memories of the siege of Londonderry and the battle of the Boyne. For them, the prospect of abandoning their relatively privileged status to become a minority group within an independent, predominantly Catholic Ireland, was intolerable. When the British prime minister, H.H. Asquith, introduced a Home Rule Bill in 1911, Ulster found in Edward Carson, MP for Trinity College, a leader who was prepared to threaten civil war, using the slogan "Ulster will fight, and Ulster will be right". It is possible that a more conciliatory line might have been taken if the Ulstermen had felt they were on their own; but from the beginning they were unscrupulously encouraged by the Conservative Party. Conservatives had always been hostile to Home Rule; in fact, during this period they should properly speaking be called Unionists, having merged with the anti-Home-Rule wing of the Liberal Party. Furthermore, stirring up trouble in Ireland was a useful tactic for an opposition party, and the Conservatives had not hesitated to "play the Orange card" in the past – to play on Protestant fears in order to embarrass Liberal governments. Now they went even further. Despite their stance as the party of law and order, they publicly backed the Ulstermen's right to use force in opposing Home Rule; and when Carson founded a paramilitary organization, the Ulster Volunteers, Conservative money and arms helped to make it a formidable sectarian army.

WE WON'T HAVE HOME RULE

COL. WALLACE · SIR EDWARD CARSON, K.C.,M.P. · CAPTAIN CRAIG, M.P.

OUR CIVIL AND RELIGIOUS · LIBERTIES WE WILL MAINTAIN

KING WILLIAM III

Anti-Home-Rule propaganda. Home Rule would have meant a self-governing Ireland in which Catholics comprised a majority. Led by Sir Edward Carson (central portrait), Protestant Ulster therefore prepared to resist Home Rule – if necessary, by force. The figure of William III, still a hero and model more than two centuries after the battle of the Boyne, demonstrates the way in which memories and myths of the past continued to influence Irish politics.

Mutiny at the Curragh

Asquith's Liberal government took no effective action against the Ulster Volunteers, and behaved even more feebly when confronted by support for the Orangemen in the British army. In March 1914 Brigadier-General Hubert Gough and fifty-seven cavalry officers at the Curragh Camp announced that, if ordered to take military action against Ulster, they would refuse. This, "the Mutiny at the Curragh", went unpunished. And a month later, 20,000 rifles and three million rounds of ammunition from Germany were run into the North and distributed to the Ulster Volunteers without any significant opposition on the part of the authorities. Whether Asquith's passive attitude was wise from a British point of view (civil war, mutiny and/or mass resignations from the army were not attractive prospects at any time, let alone in 1914) is debatable; but it was bound to suggest to Irish nationalists that the government might not go through with Home Rule. Even the granting of Home Rule did not decide the issue, since the legislation was immediately shelved for the duration of the war; and, furthermore, Asquith assured parliament that Home Rule would not be forced on Ulster, or even implemented without provisions allowing the North to opt out for some undetermined period of time.

The growth of separatist feeling

By the 1880s the overwhelming majority of Irishmen spoke English, not Gaelic, and in most respects resembled men and women across the Irish Channel. But a group of Irish activists – most, but not all of them Catholics – set themselves to re-create a more distinct national identity, and achieved a surprising degree of success. The Gaelic Athletic Association promoted traditional Irish games such as hurley, and had an influence on many young people that went far beyond sport. And in 1893 the Gaelic League began to campaign vigorously for a revival of the Gaelic language. Although only a minority of the population were touched by these activities, they did lay the basis for the development of a more separatist, even anti-British mentality, if the political situation should deteriorate. Paradoxically, this was also the period of the Irish Literary Revival, marked by the appearance of great poets and playwrights such as W.B. Yeats and J.M. Synge, who wrote on Irish subjects but employed the English language to do so.

The nationalists arm

The Home Rule controversy and the founding of the Ulster Volunteers prompted a more political and militant response among Irish nationalists. In November 1913 the Irish Volunteers were founded by Eoin MacNeill, a professor at the (Catholic) National University, who was also the driving force behind the Gaelic League. The Volunteers began as a self-defence force in reaction to the Ulster Volunteers, but soon became identified with revolutionary republicanism. (The Irish Citizen Army, which was to become the Irish Volunteers' partner in the rising, originated in response to a different kind of crisis, a great labour dispute in 1913, during which demonstrators had been brutally assaulted by the police.) Like their Ulster equivalents, the Irish Volunteers had run guns into the country (in July 1914), though in much smaller quantities, and had successfully foiled the authorities' strenuous efforts to prevent their distribution. In this and

53

Mrs Erskine Childers and the Hon. Mary Spring-Rice aboard the yacht Asgard. In response to the arming of Ulster, these nationalists successfully ran German guns and ammunition into Howth, from where they were distributed to sympathizers in various parts of the country.

other instances, the nationalists' anger was fuelled by the contrast between official attitudes towards their activities and towards those of the Orangemen.

Ireland in the World War

Nevertheless, most nationalist Irishmen still retained a good deal of faith in the parliamentary party and the promise of Home Rule. And although it involved the suspension of the Home Rule Act, the outbreak of the First World War actually made the majority of Irishmen less politically militant. Many thousands volunteered to join the British army, encouraged by Redmond, who believed that a show of loyalty to the Crown would ensure Home Rule for a united Ireland. The war itself brought prosperity, since the army absorbed the unemployed, separation money and similar benefits eased the lot of their wives and children, and wartime needs set up a demand for agricultural goods and stimulated industrial development. A fortnight before the Easter Rising, the Director of Military Intelligence in Ireland reported that "The mass of the people are sound and loyal as regards the war, and the country is in a very prosperous state."

The Volunteers divided

MacNeill also recognized this, and said so forcibly: "The only possible basis for successful revolutionary action is

This First World War recruiting poster attempts to win Irish sympathies for Britain and her allies by picturing a German atrocity, the sinking of the British liner Lusitania, *1,153 of whose passengers lost their lives. Hundreds of thousands of Irishmen did in fact serve in the British armed forces.*

widespread popular discontent. We have only to look around us in the streets to realize that no such condition exists in Ireland." He and other important figures in the Irish Volunteers, including The O'Rahilly and Bulmer Hobson, were therefore opposed to an immediate resort to arms. It was no accident that those who disagreed – men like Pearse, Plunkett, MacDermott and Clarke – had identical views on what should be done: unknown to MacNeill, they formed a cohesive faction within the Volunteers, since they were all members of the secret Irish Republican Brotherhood (IRB), which exercised an unseen influence within most nationalist organizations. Believing that the British would soon arrest all the nationalist leaders, the IRB determined to launch a rising before it was too late; and they were also conscious of the pressure being brought to bear by James Connolly, who taunted the Volunteers with their inactivity and threatened to lead his Citizen Army into action without them. Consequently, Pearse and the IRB faction made up their minds to exploit the Volunteer manoeuvres scheduled for Easter Sunday, 1916, using the occasion to start an insurrection with or without MacNeill's consent.

Orders and cancellations During the week before Easter, tensions built up within the leadership of the Volunteers, and on the Thursday MacDermott arranged the involuntary "disappearance" of Bulmer Hobson, who had got wind of Pearse's intentions. But on the Easter Friday MacDermott and MacDonagh decided to confront MacNeill with the vital information that a German steamer, the *Aud*, was on its way to Ireland, carrying quantities of munitions for the rebels. Convinced by this that a rising was now unavoidable, MacNeill felt that he had no alternative but to put his authority behind it. But shortly afterwards, when news arrived that the British had trapped the *Aud*, which had been scuttled by her captain, MacNeill concluded that this made an insurrection out of the question. Determined to prevent any kind of outbreak, he cancelled the Easter Sunday marches and manoeuvres, giving his decision the widest possible circulation by publishing it in the *Sunday Independent* newspaper; The O'Rahilly, equally determined, toured his native Kerry to make sure it would remain quiet. However, Pearse and his supporters, now in close alliance with James Connolly (who was admitted to the IRB), decided to go ahead a day later than planned, and, bypassing MacNeill, sent out orders for Volunteer units to assemble on the morning of Easter Monday.

The rising To their dismay, the rebels discovered that MacNeill's action had been all too effective. In the provinces, where communications were slow, confusion reigned. There were limited outbreaks in Meath, Galway and Louth, but in Cork, where the Irish Volunteers were particularly militant and a thousand men had mustered on the Sunday, the final instructions to take up arms arrived too late to be put into effect. News travelled faster in Dublin itself, but even there many Volunteers stayed at home, uncertain where their loyalties lay, or unsuspectingly went off on holiday. The rebels' lack of numbers determined many features of the rising, including the essentially defensive strategy of seizing strongpoints and holding them to the last. However, it is possible that a more aggressive course of action might have led to a swifter, and therefore more humiliating, defeat. And the orders and counter-orders that confused the Volunteers were not without a compensating advantage, since they also misled the British. When MacNeill issued his cancellation, the authorities relaxed; their intelligence service had penetrated the Volunteers' leadership, and they knew that the cancellation was genuine. They had not penetrated the IRB, and were therefore unaware that the rising would take place despite the decisions of the Volunteers' own leader. And so, whatever their other problems, the Volunteers and the Citizen Army were able to assemble and march off to fight in broad daylight, and yet would manage to take their enemies completely by surprise.

Was the rising a success or a failure?

"When we are all wiped out, people will condemn us and blame us for everything. But in a few years they will see the meaning of what we tried to do." Pearse's prediction seemed unlikely to be fulfilled at the end of Easter week, when the captive rebels found themselves being pelted by their fellow-Dubliners and denounced by Redmond and the Irish Party, the elected representatives of the Irish people. All the same, many Irishmen seem to have felt a residual sympathy for men who had fought for their convictions, and had put up a remarkably good fight. The poet Æ (pseudonym of George William Russell) expressed this mixed feeling, writing:

> Here's to you, Pearse, your dream, not mine.
> And yet the thought, for this you died,
> Has turned life's water into wine.

The making of martyrs

Despite their reputed admiration for a game loser, the British felt nothing but resentment and outrage: to them, the rebels were simply "pro-Germans" and "traitors". Martial law had been proclaimed on the second day of the insurrection, and so the captured republicans were tried by courts-martial. The formalities were observed in every case, and therefore the convictions and executions, always publicly announced after the event, were spread out over almost a fortnight – a drawn-out procedure that made the British reaction seem more brutal and merciless than it actually was. In all, ninety rebels were condemned to death, and of these only fifteen in fact faced the firing squad; but they were enough to have a marked effect on Irish feeling. Pearse and all the other members of the Provisional Government were shot, including the doomed, tubercular Plunkett, who was married to his fiancée four hours before his execution, and the badly wounded James Connolly. Worse, the British also shot less politically prominent men such as Willie Pearse – as it seemed, mainly because he was Patrick's brother – and Daly, Ceannt, Heuston, Mallin and others who had commanded rebel contingents to some effect.

A few months later there was another execution which kept the Easter Rising in the public mind. Sir Roger Casement, a former colonial official, who was also an Irish nationalist, had tried to get help from the Germans, and had landed in Ireland

Sir Roger Casement with German sailors in the conning-tower of the submarine that brought him back to Ireland in April 1916. He is the hatless civilian with a moustache (he was normally bearded, but had shaved to disguise himself). Landing on Easter Friday, he was captured almost at once and without a struggle. The actual reason for his return was to warn his compatriots that there was no hope of significant German help, and to persuade them not to stage a rising. The trial and execution of Casement, who had become internationally known for his humanitarian work in the Congo, created some controversy – the more so because Casement's supposed diaries, detailing his sexual adventures, were circulated by the British government to discourage eminent people from speaking out on his behalf.

from a U-boat just before the Easter Rising. He was captured at once and without a struggle, but despite his distinguished humanitarian record he was tried, convicted and hanged as a traitor.

Irish opinion shifts

From the British point of view, the executions were legally correct and justified. Casement and the rest were British subjects who had betrayed their allegiance to the Crown. The majority of Irishmen were bound to view matters in a different light, even if they disapproved of the rebels, since they regarded Britain as an occupying power whose claim to allegiance was based on force, not consent. And so the effect of the executions was to cause a revulsion in Ireland, where the dead men began to be viewed as something like martyrs, even by nationalists who did not endorse their methods. The British helped the process by interning a large number of people who were not known to have taken part in the rising, but who were judged to be potentially dangerous. Charges that British forces had committed atrocities also influenced Irish opinion in the months following the rising, especially since one incident which occurred during Easter Week was flagrant and undeniable: the execution without trial – or any shred of justification – of the journalist Francis Sheehy-Skeffington, ordered by a British officer who seems to have become mentally unbalanced as a result of his experiences on the Western Front. Since Sheehy-Skeffington happened to be a well-known Dublin character (a high-minded pacifist, feminist and socialist whom Dubliners regarded as an entertaining and harmless crank), the case made a wide impression. In this and other instances the authorities reacted (as authorities generally do) with denials, evasions, partial admissions and inconclusive official enquiries: a mixture calculated to arouse the maximum public suspicion.

The cumulative effect of British misjudgements became apparent when convicts and detainees began to be released, some of them as early as Christmas 1916. Instead of rotten fruit, they received a heroes' welcome on their return to Ireland. Anti-British feeling hardened perceptibly in 1918, when the British government became desperate for recruits to fill the gaps in the ranks made by the holocaust on the Western Front. The consequent attempt to impose conscription on Ireland had to be abandoned when it was opposed by a mass movement that further encouraged the growth of separatist feeling. The republicanism of Pearse and Connolly – a distinctly minority sentiment in 1916 – was rapidly becoming the dominant outlook among Catholic Irishmen.

Sinn Fein This was demonstrated in a series of elections, culminating in the general election of 1918, which effectively swept away the Redmondite parliamentary party. It was replaced by the Sinn Fein ("Ourselves Alone") party, founded in the early 1900s

18th June, 1917: enthusiastic crowds gather to greet the return of the first republican prisoners from English gaols. The defeated rebels had left Ireland amid general hostility, but the execution of Pearse and other leaders of the Easter Rising caused a violent turn-about in Irish opinion.

by Arthur Griffiths, whose policy was to abstain from taking the seats it had won in the British parliament at Westminster; instead, Irish MPs would set up their own national parliament and try to administer Irish affairs, cutting across British efforts to make their authority felt. Sinn Fein had taken no direct part in the Easter Rising, yet almost everyone – Irish as well as British – wrongly labelled the rebels Sinn Fein or, derisively, "Shinners". By a curious irony of history, it was *after* the rising that Sinn Fein became an important political force and in effect merged with the republican groups including rebel survivors such as Eamon de Valera. (De Valera, the senior surviving rebel commander, may well have owed his life to his American birth, which probably persuaded the British authorities that it would be embarrassing to execute him when they were hoping that the United States would enter the war on their side.) Incidentally, one of the successful Sinn Fein candidates in 1918 was Countess Markievicz, who became the first woman elected to parliament; following the Sinn Fein policy, she refused to take her seat, and it was left to Nancy Astor in 1919 to become the first sitting woman Member.

Independence and civil war

The rise of Sinn Fein was a decisive event in modern Irish history, which can only be described here in the briefest of summaries. The post-war confrontation between Sinn Fein

"Black and Tans" in action during the war between the Irish Republican Army and the British. The Black and Tans were not regular soldiers, but armed auxiliaries – technically policemen – recruited from the unemployed and from ex-servicemen who had failed to settle down after the end of the First World War. Their wild indiscipline and savage reprisals (never effectively restrained or punished by the authorities) made their name a byword in Ireland.

WAS THE RISING A SUCCESS OR A FAILURE?

Michael Collins in uniform. Collins served as an officer in the GPO during the Easter Rising. Afterwards, he quickly rose to prominence in the republican movement, becoming the ingenious, elusive leader of a sustained guerrilla war against the British. However, the compromise treaty he later signed with Britain was denounced by de Valera and others, and a bitter civil war ensued. The new Irish government, at first led by Collins, suppressed the republican rebels, but not before Collins himself had been killed in an ambush.

and the British government led to an all-out war in which more blood was shed, and more atrocities committed on both sides, than in the Easter Rebellion. The military organization set up by Sinn Fein, the Irish Republican Army (IRA), was led by Michael Collins, who had seen service in the GPO during the Easter Rising. The IRA fought a guerrilla war (1919-21) which involved a good many acts of "terrorism" answered (or provoked) by British reprisals; these were often savage, especially where the notorious "Black and Tans" – in effect British mercenaries – were involved. Finally, in December 1921, a nationalist delegation led by Collins and Griffiths settled for the best terms they believed they could get: most of Ireland became the self-governing Dominion of Eire, or Irish Free State, but the Protestant-dominated six counties of Ulster remained part of what was now to be called the United Kingdom. One wing of the Irish republican movement refused to accept this compromise, and a bitter civil war ensued between Irish government forces led by Michael Collins and rejectionists, still calling themselves the IRA, led by Eamonn de Valera. Collins himself was ambushed and killed, but the government forces were eventually victorious.

An unsolved problem

Over the next few decades, the last vestiges of the British connection were removed, and the Irish Republic was formally proclaimed in 1949. Although the IRA remained intermittently active, the majority of people in the Republic became resigned to partition, and for a time the "Irish problem" seemed to have been solved. In Ulster itself, Protestant domination was maintained and reinforced without regard for the substantial Catholic minority; but the concentration of political and economic power in Protestant hands seemed a durable if unjust arrangement, and successive British governments were content not to tamper with it.

In the late 1960s, however, a protest movement developed in the North, directed against discrimination in the way power, employment and housing were distributed. It was thus a civil rights movement, seeking justice within the "system"; and as such it was neither Catholic nor republican in its aims, although Catholics were of course the victims it sought to help. This was an imaginative attempt to avoid a conflict defined in terms of Catholic versus Protestant, but it failed to shift vested interests and entrenched Protestant attitudes, or to persuade British governments to act with sufficient speed and decision. Instead, violence increased, the Catholic/republican and Protestant/loyalist split reappeared, and the guns were drawn again. The "Irish problem" re-emerged as "the Northern Irish problem", and is still unsolved, and destroying human lives, at the time of writing.

Success? The Easter Rising succeeded in doing what Pearse hoped it would: with a little help from the British, it turned nationalist Irishmen into militant revolutionaries, determined to make their country independent. On the other hand, it is impossible to say whether the rising was a success in the sense of being "a good thing": since the alternative ("non-rising") situation never actually occurred, we cannot judge it or compare it with the rising and its effects. (This is of course true of *all* historical events.) Speculation in this area has little value except in countering the assumption that everything in history happens for the best. For example, it could be argued that the "success" of the rising was a disaster – that, if it had never taken place, the Liberals' Home Rule measures would have

Memories of the past influence the present in these posters issued by the Northern Irish republican party, Sinn Fein, and displayed in a shop window. The "salute" to Pearse, Connolly and other leaders of the Easter Rising is designed to carry a message for today. Pearse and the rest were "men of violence" – a phrase widely used by those who condemn modern Irish "para-military" groups such as the IRA, which employs violence in its efforts to drive the British army from Ulster and create a united Ireland. But Pearse and his "men of violence" are now regarded as Irish heroes – and, the poster implies, the same will prove to be true of the IRA and its "men of violence".

brought about much the same result (partition and self-government for the South) as the republican campaigns, with less bloodshed and without Irishmen experiencing the bitterness of civil war. And if this were so, the Anglo-Irish connection would have remained much closer, and the whole history of the island would have been different. Whether this – if correct – would have made the problem of Ulster any easier to solve, is another matter. The history of modern Ireland offers many might-have-beens; the Easter Rising constitutes one of its central facts.

Further reading

THE EVENTS

Thomas M. Coffey, *Agony at Easter: the 1916 Irish Uprising*, Harrap, 1970. (A detailed account of events at the General Post Office.)
Charles Duff, *Six Days to Shake an Empire*, Dent, 1966. (Describes the rising and argues that it provided a model for later anti-colonialist revolts.)
Roger McHugh (editor), *Dublin 1916*, Arlington Books, 1966. (An anthology of eye-witness accounts.)

THE INVESTIGATION

Ruth Dudley Edwards, *James Connolly*, Gill and Macmillan, 1981
Constantine Fitzgibbon, *Out of the Lion's Paw: Ireland wins Her Freedom*, Macdonald, 1969
Kenneth Griffith and Timothy E. O'Grady, *Curious Journey: An Oral History of Ireland's Unfinished Revolution*, Hutchinson, 1982
Robert Kee, *The Green Flag*, Quartet
Lord Longford and Thomas P. O'Neill, *Eamon de Valera*, Hutchinson, 1970
F.S.L. Lyons, *Ireland Since the Famine*, Weidenfeld, 1971
Ulick O'Connor, *A Terrible Beauty is Born: The Irish Troubles 1912-1922*, Hamish Hamilton, 1975; Granada paperback, 1981

Index

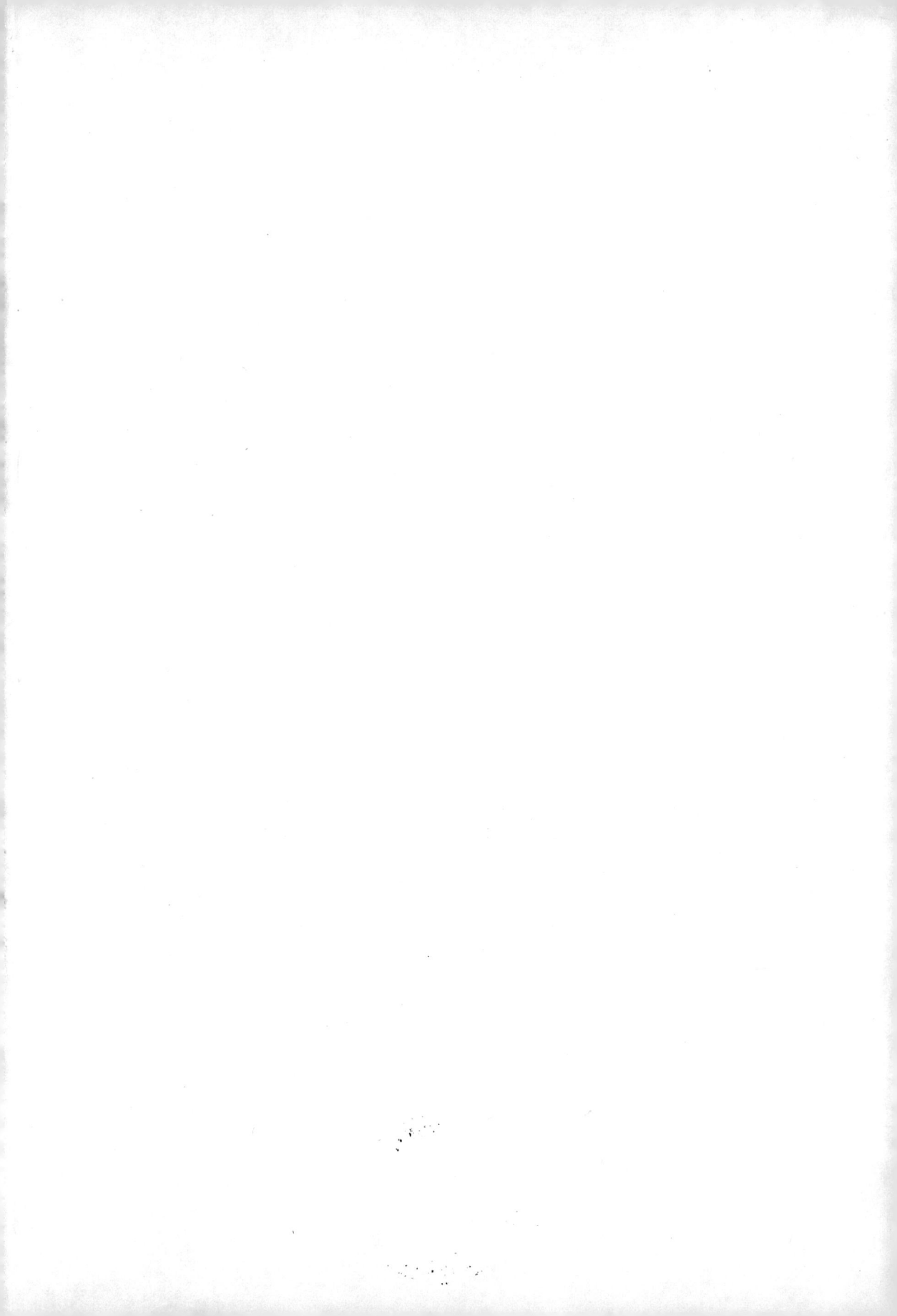